CW00468777

AIR FRYER COOKBOOK

Beginner-
Friendly Recipes with Handy Tips & Techniques for Frying, Gri
lling, Roasting and Baking | The Essential Guide to Air Fried C
ooking for Everyday Meals

by

Adelina Astra Rocha

All rights reserved. No part of this publication may be re produced, stored, or transmitted in any form or by any m eans, electronic, mechanical, photocopying, recording, sc anning, or otherwise without written permission from th e author. It is illegal to copy this book, post it to a website , or distribute it by any other means without permission.

© 2023 Adelina Astra Rocha. The year of publication of t he book. The name of the owner of the works, which is us ually the author or publishing house name.

Readers usually ignore one of the most important pages i n the book: the copyright page. In a physical book, it's us ually printed on the back of the title page. In an e-Book, it comes right after the title page.

You own the copyright to your book the moment you begi n writing it. But if you want to safeguard your copyright, you need to do more. By registering the copyright to your book with the U.S. Copyright Office, you protect your abil ity to enforce your rights over your book against any infri ngement of those rights.

Introduction

Welcome to our Air Fryer Cookbook, a culinary guide that will take your cooking experience to new heights with the revolutionary air frying technique. This cookbook is designed to help you explore the endless possibilities of creating delicious, crispy, and healthier meals using your air fryer.

The air fryer has gained immense popularity in recent years due to its ability to replicate the crispy texture of deep-fried foods using significantly less oil. It works by circulating hot air around the food, creating a crispy exterior while retaining moisture and tenderness inside. This method not only produces satisfying results but also reduces the amount of unhealthy fats typically associated with deep frying.

In this cookbook, you will discover a wide variety of recipes that showcase the versatility of the air fryer. From appetizers and snacks to main courses and even desserts, the air fryer opens up a world of possibilities for creating flavorful and wholesome meals with less oil and fewer calories.

By using your air fryer to prepare meals, you can enjoy the indulgence of crispy and crunchy textures without sacrificing your health or compromising on taste. The recipes in this cookbook have been carefully crafted to optimize the use of the air fryer, ensuring that you achieve the desired texture and flavor in each dish.

Not only does the air fryer provide healthier cooking options, but it also offers convenience and efficiency. With its quick preheating time and shorter cooking durations, the air fryer can help you prepare meals in a fraction of the time compared to traditional cooking methods. It's a fantastic tool for busy individuals and families looking for convenient yet delicious meal solutions.

Whether you're a seasoned air fryer enthusiast or just starting to explore the possibilities, this cookbook will guide you through the process with clear instructions, helpful tips, and a range of delectable recipes. You'll find inspiration for breakfasts, lunches, dinners, and even snacks that showcase the versatility of this remarkable appliance.

Get ready to embark on a culinary adventure, experimenting with flavors, textures, and innovative cooking techniques. The air fryer opens up a whole new world of healthy and tasty possibilities, allowing you to enjoy your favorite foods guilt-free.

So, let's dive into the world of air frying and unlock the potential of your air fryer with this cookbook. Get ready to savor crispy, flavorful, and healthier meals that will satisfy your taste buds and elevate your cooking game.

Air Fryer Cookbook Benefits

An Air Fryer Cookbook offers several benefits for individuals who want to explore healthier cooking options and enjoy delicious meals. Here are some key advantages :

Healthier Cooking with Less Oil: The main benefit of an air fryer is that it allows you to achieve a crispy and crunchy texture similar to deep-fried foods but with significantly less oil. By using hot air circulation and a minimal amount of oil, an air fryer can produce crispy and delicious results, reducing the overall fat content of your meals. This can contribute to a healthier diet and weight management.

Reduced Calorie Intake: By using an air fryer to cook your favorite dishes, you can significantly reduce the calorie content compared to deep-frying or using oil-laden cooking methods. The air fryer eliminates the need for excessive oil, resulting in meals that are lower in calories without compromising on taste and texture. This can be particularly beneficial for those looking to lose weight or maintain a healthy weight.

Versatile Cooking Options: An air fryer cookbook provides a wide range of recipes that can be prepared using the air frying technique. From appetizers and main courses to snacks and desserts, the versatility of an air fryer allows you to explore various culinary creations. You can enjoy crispy fries, chicken wings, roasted vegetables, fish fillets, and even baked goods, all prepared with the air fryer's unique cooking method.

Time and Energy Efficiency: Air fryers are known for their quick preheating time and shorter cooking durations compared to conventional ovens or stovetop cooking. This means you can prepare meals faster, saving both time and energy. The air fryer's efficiency is especially beneficial for busy individuals or those who prefer quick and hassle-free cooking.

Convenience and Easy Cleanup: Cooking with an air fryer is generally a straightforward process. It often involves setting the temperature, adjusting the cooking time, and letting the air fryer do its job. Many air fryer accessories and cooking baskets are also dishwasher-safe, making cleanup a breeze. This convenience and ease of use make the air fryer an appealing option for those who want to simplify their cooking routine.

Retains Nutritional Value: The air frying technique helps to retain the nutritional value of the ingredients used in your meals. The hot air circulation cooks food quickly and evenly, helping to preserve vitamins, minerals, and other essential nutrien ts. This ensures that your meals not only taste great but also provide the nutritional benefits you seek from your ingredients.

Table of Contents

BONUS 91

BREAKFAST

Air Fryer Carrot Coffee Cake

Preparation Time: 15 minutes | **Cooking Time:** 35 minutes | Serves: 6

Ingredients:

- 1/3 cup walnuts, chopped and toasted
- 1 large egg, lightly beaten, lukewarm
- 1/4 cup cranberries, dried
- 1/2 cup buttermilk
- 1 cup carrots, shredded
- 1/3 cup sugar and 2 tbsp. sugar, divided 1/4 tsp salt
- 3 tbsp. canola oil 1/4 tsp baking soda
- 2 tbsp. dark brown sugar
- 2 tsp pumpkin pie spice, divided 1 tsp orange zest, grated
- 1/3 cup white whole wheat flour 1 tsp vanilla extract
- 2/3 cup all-purpose flour 1 tsp baking powder

Instructions:

1. Preheat the air fryer to 350 F. Grease and flour a round baking pan of 6 inches. Whisk vanilla, orange zest, brown sugar, oil, 1/3 cup of sugar, buttermilk and egg i n a large bowl. Whisk the flours, salt, 1 teaspoon of pumpkin pie spice and baking powder in a separate. Gradually beat the contents into the egg mixture. Then fold i n dried cranberries and carrots. Transfer into the prepared pan.

2. Combine the remaining one teaspoon of pumpkin spice, 2 tablespoons of sugar a nd walnuts in a small bowl. Drizzle evenly on top of batter. Carefully put the pan i nto a large air fryer basket.

3. Air fry for about 35 to 40 minutes until a toothpick comes out clean when insert ed at the center. If the top is too dark, tightly cover with foil. Let to cool for 10 min utes in pan on a wire rack before transferring from pan. Serve while still warm.

Nutritional values:

Calories: 316 | Carbohydrates: 46g | Cholesterol: 32mg | Fat: 13g | Saturated Fat : 1g | Sodium: 297mg | Fiber: 3g | Protein: 6g | Sugars: 27g

Air Fryer French Toast Sticks

Preparation Time: 20 minutes | **Cooking Time:** 10 minutes | Serves: 2

Ingredients:

- Maple syrup
- 6 slices day-old Texas toast Confectioners' sugar, if desired 4 eggs, large
- 1 cup cornflakes (crushed), if desired 1 cup 2 percent milk
- 1 tsp vanilla extract 2 tbsp. sugar
- 1/4 to 1/2 tsp ground cinnamon

Instructions:

1. Slice each piece of bread into thirds. Transfer to an ungreased dish of 13x9-in. Whisk the eggs, cinnamon, vanilla, sugar and milk in a large bowl. Spread on b read. Soak for two minutes and flip once. Coat the bread on all sides with cornflake crumbs.

2. Transfer into a greased baking pan of 15x10x1-in. Place in a freezer for around 45 minutes until firm. Transfer to a resealable fre ezer bag or an airtight container and then store in your freezer.

3. Using frozen French toast sticks: Preheat the air fryer to 350 degrees F. Arrange the sticks on a greased tray in the basket. Air fry for 3 minutes. Flip and continue to cook for 2 to 3 minutes until golden brown. If desired, drizzle with confectioners' sugar. Serve with syrup.

Nutritional values:

Calories: 184 | Carbohydrates: 24g | Cholesterol: 128mg | Fat: 6g | Saturated Fat : 2g | Sodium: 253mg | Fiber: 1g | Protein: 8g | Sugars: 8g

Cheesy Breakfast Egg Rolls

Preparation Time: 30 minutes | **Cooking Time:** 10 minutes | Serves: 12

Ingredients:

- ½ cup shredded sharp cheddar cheese 12 egg roll wrappers
- 1 tbsp. 2 percent milk 1 tbsp. butter
- ½ cup Monterey Jack cheese, shredded 1/8 tsp pepper
- 1 tbsp. green onions, chopped ¼ tsp salt
- 4 large eggs

Instructions:

1. Over medium heat, cook the sausage while breaking into crumbles in a nonstick skillet for 4 to 6 minutes until pink color disappears. Add green onions and cheeses . Reserve. Wipe the skillet until it's clean.

2. Whisk the milk, eggs, pepper and salt in a small bowl until blended. Over mediu m heat, melt butter in the same skillet. Add the egg mixture and cook while stirrin g until no liquid egg remains and the eggs are thickened. Add sausage mixture and stir.

3. Preheat the air fryer to 400 degrees F. Set one corner of the egg roll wrapper to point towards you. Pour ¼ cup of filling below the middle of the wrapper. (Use a da mp paper towel to cover the remaining wrappers until when ready to use.) Fold the bottom corner over the filling and then moisten the rest of the wrapper edges with water. Fold the side corners towards the middle over the filling. Tightly roll up the egg roll and seal by pressing at the tip. Repeat this process with the remaining wr appers.

4. Working in batches, spread the egg rolls on a greased tray in the fryer basket an d drizzle cooking spray. Air fry for 3 to 4 minutes. Flip and sprinkle with cooking s pray. Continue to cook for 3 to 4 minutes until crisp and golden brown. You can ser ve with salsa or maple syrup if you like.

Nutritional values:

Calories: 209 | Carbohydrates: 19g | Cholesterol: 87mg | Fat: 10g | Saturated Fat : 4g | Sodium: 438mg | Fiber: 1g | Protein: 10g

Air Fryer French Toast Cups with Raspberries

Preparation Time: 20 minutes | **Cooking Time:** 20 minutes | Serves: 2

Ingredients:

- 1 tbsp. maple syrup
- 2 slices of Italian bread, chop into half-inch cubes 1/2 cup whole milk
- 1/2 cup raspberries (fresh or frozen) 2 large eggs
- 2 ounces cream cheese, chop into half-inch cubes

Raspberry syrup

- Ground cinnamon, if desired 2 tsp cornstarch
- ½ tsp lemon zest, grated 1/3 cup water
- 1 tbsp. lemon juice
- 2 cups raspberries (fresh or frozen), divided 1 tbsp. maple syrup

Instructions:

1. Divide ½ of the bread cubes between two greased custard cups of 8-oz. Drizzle with cream cheese and raspberries. Add the remaining bread on top. Whisk syrup, milk and eggs in a small bowl. Pour on top of bread. Cover and then chill in your fridge for at least an hour.

2. Preheat the air fryer appliance to 325 degrees F. Transfer the custard cups to the tray of your fryer basket. Air fry for about 12 to 15 minutes until puffed and golden brown.

3. In the meantime, mix together the water and cornstarch in a small saucepan until smooth. Pour in 1-1/2 cups of raspberries, lemon zest, syrup and lemon juice. Heat to boil and then lower the heat. Cook while stirring for two minutes until thickened. Strain and get rid of seeds. Let to cool a little.

4. Carefully stir the remaining half cup of berries into the syrup. Drizzle cinnamon onto French toast cups if desired. Serve along with syrup.

Nutritional values:

Calories: 406 | Carbohydrates: 50g | Cholesterol: 221mg | Fat: 18g | Saturated Fat: 8g | Sodium: 301mg | Fiber: 11g | Protein: 14g | Sugars: 24g

Air Fryer Breakfast Croquettes with Egg & Asparagus

Preparation Time: 30 minutes | **Cooking Time:** 15 minutes | **Servings:** 6

Ingredients:

- Cooking spray 3 tbsp. butter
- 3 large beaten eggs
- 1-3/4 cups panko bread crumbs
- 3 tbsp. all-purpose flour
- 1/4 tsp pepper
- 3/4 cup 2 percent milk 1/4 tsp salt
- 6 large eggs, hard-boiled & chopped
- 1 tbsp. fresh tarragon minced
- ½ cup fresh asparagus, slice
- 1/3 cup cheddar cheese, shredded
- ½ cup green onions, sliced

Instructions:

1. Over medium heat, melt the butter in a large saucepan. Add flour and stir until smooth. Cook while stirring for 1 to 2 minutes until browned lightly. Slowly whisk in the milk. Cook while stirring until the mixture is thickened. Add tarragon, chees e, pepper, salt, green onions, asparagus and hard-boiled eggs. Chill for at least two hours.

2. Preheat the air fryer to a temperature of 350 F. Shape ¼ cupfuls of the egg mixt ure into 12 long ovals of 3-in. Place eggs and bread crumbs in different shallow bowls. Roll the logs in crumbs to coat and dunk in the egg. Roll once again in crumbs and pat to help coating adh ere.

3. Working in batches, arrange the croquettes on a greased tray in the fryer basket in a single layer. Drizzle with cooking spray. Air fry for 8 to 10 minutes until gold en brown. Flip and drizzle with cooking spray. Continue to cook for 3 to 5 minutes until golden brown.

Nutritional values:

Calories: 294 | Carbohydrates: 18g | Cholesterol: 303mg | Fat: 17g | Saturated F at: 8g | Sodium: 348mg | Fiber: 1g | Protein: 15g | Sugars: 3g

Air Fryer Breakfast Sweet Potato Skins

Preparation Time: 7 minutes | **Cooking Time:** 23 minutes | **Servings:** 4

Ingredients:

- 1 small sliced tomato
- 2 green chopped onions 4 slices of cooked bacon Pepper and salt
- 4 eggs
- 2 teaspoons olive oil ¼ cup whole milk
- 2 medium sweet potatoes

Instructions:

1. Clean sweet potatoes and then add 3 to 4 cuts to the potatoes. Heat in microwave for 6 to 8 minutes, depends on the size, until soft.

2. Cut potatoes in half lengthwise with an oven mitt. Scoop potato flesh out and leave ¼-in. around the edges. Set aside scooped potato for another use.

3. Brush olive oil onto the potato skins and drizzle with sea salt. Place skins in your fryer basket and air fry for 10 minutes at 400 F.

4. In the meantime, add the milk, eggs, pepper and salt to non-stick skillet. Over medium heat, cook the mix while stirring continuously until no liquid eggs is visible.

5. Add a slice of crumbled bacon and ¼ of scrambled eggs onto each cooked potato skin. Top with shredded cheese. Place back into the basket of your air fryer and let to cook at 400 F for 3 minutes or until cheese has melted.

6. Top with tomato and green onion and serve.

Nutritional values:

Calories: 208 | Carbohydrates: 14g | Cholesterol: 7g | Fat: 12g | Saturated Fat: 4g | Sodium: 199mg | Fiber: 2g | Protein: 12g

Air Fryer Breakfast Cookies

Preparation Time: 20 minutes | **Cooking Time:** 10 minutes | **Servings:** 2

Ingredients:

- 1 cup raisins or cranberries, dried
- 1 cup ripe bananas, mashed (about 2 medium) ¼ tsp baking soda
- ½ cup chunky peanut butter ½ tsp salt
- ½ cup honey
- 2 tsp ground cinnamon 1 tsp vanilla extract
- ¼ cup nonfat dry milk powder ½ cup whole wheat flour
- 1 cup old-fashioned oats

Instructions:

1. Preheat the air fryer to a temperature of 300 F. In a bowl, beat vanilla, honey, peanut butter and banana until blended. Mix baking soda, salt, cinnamon, milk powder, flour and oats in a second bowl. Then slowly beat into the banana mixture. Add dried cranberries and stir.

2. Working in batches, pour the dough by ¼ cupfuls on a greased tray in the fryer basket two inches apart. Form into half inch thickness.

3. Air fry for 6 to 8 minutes until browned lightly. Let to cool in the basket for a minute. Transfer to wire racks.

4. Serve while still warm or at lukewarm.

5. Freeze option: Place the cookies in freezer containers and freeze. Ensure you separate layers with waxed paper. When planning to use, thaw prior to serving or if you like, reheat in an air fryer preheated to 300 F for about a minute until warmed.

Nutritional values:

Calories: 212 | Carbohydrates: 38g | Fat: 6g | Saturated Fat: 1g | Sodium: 186mg | Fiber: 4g | Protein: 5g | Sugars: 25g

Air Fryer Candied Bacon

Preparation Time: 5 minutes | **Cooking Time:** 18 minutes | **Servings:** 12

Ingredients:

- 8 ounces of thick cut bacon 1 tbsp. rice wine vinegar
- 6 tbsp. maple syrup or honey ¼ cup white miso paste
- 1 tbsp. butter

Instructions:

1. Preheat your air fryer to 390 degrees F.

2. Over medium heat, melt butter in a small saucepan. Adjust the heat to medium-high and then pour in rice wine vinegar, honey and miso paste. Stir till the Ingredients are well combined. Bring to boil. Transfer from the heat source and reserve.

3. Spread bacon in a single layer in the basket. Avoid overlapping. Cook for about 3 to 4 minutes per side. Smear a thin layer of miso glaze on one side of bacon with a pastry brush. Cook for one more minute. The bacon should be sticky and crispy.

Nutritional values:

Calories: 131 | Carbohydrates: 10g | Cholesterol: 15mg | Fat: 9g | Saturated Fat: 3g | Sodium: 347mg | Protein: 3g

Air Fryer Toad-In-The-Hole

Preparation Time: 10 minutes | **Cooking Time:** 25 minutes | **Servings:** 4

Ingredients:

- 1/8 tsp pepper 1/8 tsp salt
- 2 eggs, large
- 1 tsp stone-ground mustard 1 cup 2 percent milk
- 1 tsp onion powder
- 1/2 cup all-purpose flour

Instructions:

1. Preheat the air fryer to a temperature of 400 F. Slice the sausages in half width wise. Place in a 6-

in. baking pan that is greased. Transfer the pan on the tray in the air fryer basket. Air fry for 6 to 8 minutes, flipping once, until browned lightly.

2. In the meantime, whisk the milk, eggs, mustard, pepper, salt and onion powder. Stir in bacon if desired. Add onto the sausages. Cook for about 10 to 15 minutes un til golden brown and puffed. Serve right away. Garnish with parsley if desired.

Nutritional values:

Calories: 257 | Carbohydrates: 16g | Cholesterol: 143mg | Fat: 15g | Saturated F at: 5g | Sodium: 494mg | Fiber: 1g | Protein: 16g | Sugars: 3g

Air Fryer Ham & Cheese Breakfast Bundles

Preparation Time: 35 minutes | **Cooking Time:** 10 minutes | **Servings:** 4

Ingredients:

- 2 tsp chives, minced
- 5 sheets phyllo dough (14x9 inches) 2 tsp seasoned bread crumbs
- 1/4 cup melted butter
- 1/4 cup provolone cheese, shredded
- 2 ounces cream cheese, slice into 4 pieces 1/4 cup cooked ham, fully chopped
- 4 eggs, large 1/8 tsp pepper 1/8 tsp salt

Instructions:

1. Preheat the air fryer to 325 degrees F. On a work surface, place one sheet of the phyllo dough. Rub with butter. Lay 4 more phyllo sheets and brush each layer. (Cover the remaining phyllo with a damp towel to prevent them from drying out.) Slice the layered sheets crosswise in half and then slice lengthwise in half.

2. Transfer each stack into a greased ramekin of 4-oz. Add a piece of cream cheese to fill each. Gently break 1 egg into each cup. Drizzle with pepper and salt. Top with chives, bread crumbs, cheese and ham. Bring the phyllo together above the filling. Seal by pinching and form bundles.

3. Transfer the ramekins on the tray in the basket and smear with the remaining butter. Air fry for 10 to 12 minutes until golden brown. Serve while still warm.

Nutritional values:

Calories: 301 | Carbohydrates: 10g | Cholesterol: 241mg | Fat: 24g | Saturated Fat: 13g | Sodium: 522mg | Protein: 12g | Sugars: 1g

LUNCH

Air Fryer Southern-Style Chicken

Preparation Time: 15 minutes | **Cooking Time:** 20 minutes | **Servings:** 6

Ingredients:

- 1 fryer/broiler chicken, about 3-
  4 pounds, chopped up 2 cups Ritz crackers, crushed (about 50)
- 1 large beaten egg Cooking spray
- ¼ tsp rubbed sage ½ tsp pepper
- 1 tsp paprika
- ¼ tsp cumin, ground 1 tbsp. garlic salt
- 1 tbsp. parsley, fresh and minced

Instructions:

1. Preheat the air fryer appliance to 375 F. Combine the parsley, Ritz crackers, gar lic salt, sage, cumin, pepper and paprika in a shallow bowl. Crack the egg in anoth er shallow bowl. Dunk the chicken in the egg, and then dip in the cracker mixture. Pat to ensure the coating adheres. Working in batches, put the meat on the grease d tray in the air fryer basket in a single layer. Drizzle with cooking spray.

2. Let to cook for ten minutes. Flip the chicken and then drizzle cooking spray on t op. Continue to cook the for about 10 to 20 minutes until the juices run clear and t he meat turns golden brown.

Nutritional values:

Chicken 5 ounces: Calories: 410 | Carbohydrates: 2g | Cholesterol: 135 mg | Fat: 23g | Saturated Fat: 6g | Sodium: 460mg | Fiber: 1g | Protein: 36g | Sugars: 2g

Air Fryer Sweet and Sour Pork

Preparation Time: 25 minutes | **Cooking Time:** 15 minutes | **Servings:** 2

Ingredients:

- Cooking spray
- Unsweetened crushed pineapple (undrained) - ½ cup Chopped green onions, if desired
- Cider vinegar - ½ cup
- Pork tenderloin (3/4 pound), halved - 1 Sugar - 1/4 cup
- Garlic powder - ½ tsp
- Dark brown sugar (packed) - 1/4 cup Reduced-sodium soy sauce - 1 tbsp. Ketchup - 1/4 cup
- Dijon mustard – 1 to ½ tsp Pepper - 1/8 tsp
- Salt - 1/8 tsp

Instructions:

1. Mix the garlic powder, Dijon mustard, soy sauce, ketchup, brown sugar, sugar, cider vinegar and pineapple in a small saucepan. Bring to boil and then reduce heat. Let to simmer while uncovered for 6 to 8 minutes, stirring frequently, until thickened.

2. Preheat the air fryer to 350 degrees F. Season the pork with pepper and salt. Arrange the pork on a greased tray in the fryer basket and drizzle with cooking spray. Cook the pork for 7 to 8 minutes until it starts to brown around the edges. Flip and add two tablespoons of the sauce on top of pork. Continue to cook for 10 to 12 minutes until the internal temperature reaches at least 145 degrees F. Leave the pork to sit for 5 minutes before slicing. Serve along with the remaining sauce. Top with chopped green onions if desired.

Nutritional values:

Calories: 502 | Carbohydrates: 72g | Cholesterol: 95mg | Fat: 7g | Saturated Fat: 2g | Sodium: 985mg | Fiber: 1g | Protein: 35g

Air Fryer Steak Fajitas

Preparation Time: 15 minutes | **Cooking Time:** 8-11 minutes | **Servings:** 6

Ingredients:

1 large onion (halved and chopped)

2 large tomatoes (seeded and chopped)

1 beef flank steak (approximately 1 to ½ pounds) 1/2 cup red onion, diced

3/4 tsp salt, divided

3 tbsp. cilantro, minced and fresh 1/4 cup lime juice

2 tsp ground cumin, divided

1 jalapeno pepper

Instructions:

1. For the salsa, put the minced cilantro, jalapeno pepper, lime juice, red onion and
 tomatoes in a small bowl. Add ¼ teaspoon of salt and 1 teaspoon of cumin and stir
 . Let to sit until serving.

2. Preheat the air fryer to a temperature of 400 F. Drizzle the steak with the remai
ning salt and cumin. Transfer steak onto a greased tray in the basket of air fryer.
Cook for 6 to 8 minutes on each side until the meat reaches your desired doneness.
 For a medium-
rare, the internal temperature should reach 135 degrees, medium should be 140 F
and medium-
well should be 145 F. Transfer from the basket and allow to sit for 5 minutes.

3. In the meantime, put the onion on the tray of fryer basket. Cook for 2 to 3 minut
es, stirring once, until they're crisp-
tender. Thinly slice the steak across the grain. Then serve in tortillas along with sa
lsa and onion. You can serve with lime wedges and avocado if you like.

Nutritional values:

Calories: 309 | Carbohydrates: 29g | Cholesterol: 54mg | Fat: 9g | Saturated Fat:
4g | Sodium: 498mg | Fiber: 5g | Protein: 27g | Sugars: 69g

Air Fryer Keto Meatballs

Preparation Time: 30 minutes | **Cooking Time:** 10 minutes | **Servings:** 4

Ingredients:

- 1 pound lean ground beef, 90 percent lean 1/2 cup Parmesan cheese, grated
- 1 minced garlic clove
- 1/2 cup mozzarella cheese, shredded 2 tbsp. heavy whipping cream
- 1 large egg (beaten lightly)
- Sauce
- ¼ cup heavy whipping cream 2 tbsp. prepared pesto
- 8 ounces (1 can) tomato sauce with oregano, garlic, and basil

Instructions:

1. Preheat the air fryer to 350 degrees F. Mix the garlic clove, whipping cream, lightly beaten egg, mozzarella cheese and parmesan cheese in a large bowl. Place in beef and combine lightly but thoroughly. Form into 1 to ½ inch balls. Arrange on a greased tray in the fryer basket in a single layer. Cook for 8to 10 minutes until they're cooked through and browned lightly.

2. In the meantime, combine the sauce Ingredients in a small saucepan and heat through. Serve along with meatballs.

3. Freeze option: Place cooled meatballs in freezer containers and transfer to a freezer. When planning to use, partially thaw in a fridge overnight. Preheat your air fryer to a temperature of 350 F. Then reheat for 3 to 5 minutes until heated through. Prepared the sauce as instructed.

Nutritional values:

Calories: 404 | Carbohydrates: 7g | Cholesterol: 162mg | Fat: 27g | Saturated Fat: 13g | Sodium: 799mg | Fiber: 1g | Protein: 31g | Sugars: 3g

Air Fryer Taco Twists

Preparation Time: 15 minutes | **Cooking Time:** 20 minutes | **Servings:** 4

Ingredients:

- 8 ounces, 1 tube chilled crescent rolls 1/3 pound beef, ground
- 1/8 tsp cumin, ground 1 large sliced onion 1/4 tsp garlic powder 1/8 tsp salt
- 2/3 cup cheddar cheese, shredded 1/4 tsp hot pepper sauce
- 1/3 cup salsa
- 3 tbsp. canned sliced green chiles

Instructions:

1. Preheat the air fryer to 300 F. Over medium heat, cook onion and beef in a large skillet until the pink color in meat disappears. Drain. Mix in cumin, salt, hot pepper sauce, garlic powder, chiles, salsa and cheese.

2. Start to unroll the crescent dough and divide into 4 rectangles. Press the perforations to seal. Bring four corners to the middle and then twist. Seal by pinching. Working in batches, arrange on a greased tray in the fryer basket in a single layer. Cook for about 18 to 22 minutes until golden brown. If you want, you can serve with your favorite toppings.

Nutritional values:

Calories: 371 | Carbohydrates: 21g | Cholesterol: 42mg | Fat: 21g | Saturated Fat : 5g | Sodium: 752mg | Fiber: 1g | Protein: 16g | Sugars: 8g

Air Fryer Ham And Egg Pockets

Preparation Time: 15 minutes | **Cooking Time:** 8-10 minutes | **Servings:** 2

Ingredients:

- 4 ounces (1 tube) chilled crescent rolls 1 egg, large
- 2 tbsp. cheddar cheese (shredded) 1 ounce thinly chopped deli ham 2 tsp butter
- 2 tsp 2 percent milk

Instructions:

1. Preheat the air fryer to 300 F. Combine together the milk and egg in a small bowl. Melt butter in a small skillet until hot. Pour in the egg mixture. Over medium heat, cook while stirring until the eggs set completely. Transfer from the heat source. Fold in cheese and ham.

2. Divide the crescent dough into two rectangles. Seal all the perforations. Pour ½ of the filling in the middle of each rectangle. Then fold the dough over the filling. Seal by pinching. Arrange on a greased tray in the fryer basket in a single layer. Air fry for 8 to 10 minutes until golden brown.

Nutritional values:

Calories: 326 | Carbohydrates: 25g | Cholesterol: 118mg | Fat: 20g | Saturated Fat: 5g | Sodium: 735mg | Protein: 12g | Sugars: 6g

Air Fryer General Tso's Cauliflower

Preparation Time: 25 minutes | **Cooking Time:** 20 minutes | **Servings:** 4

Ingredients:

- 1 medium head cauliflower, chop into 1-inch florets (approx. 6 cups) ½ cup all-purpose flour
- ¾ cup club soda ½ cup cornstarch
- 1 tsp baking powder 1 tsp salt
- Sauce
- 4 cups hot cooked rice ¼ cup orange juice
- ½ tsp orange zest, grated
- 1 tsp fresh gingerroot, grated 3 tbsp. sugar
- 3 minced garlic cloves 3 tbsp. soy sauce
- 3 green onions, green part thinly chopped, white part minced 3 tbsp. vegetable broth
- 2-6 dried pasilla or any other hot chiles (chopped) 2 tsp cornstarch
- 2 tbsp. rice vinegar 2 tbsp. canola oil
- 2 tsp sesame oil

Instructions:

1. Preheat the air fryer to 400 degrees F. Mix the baking powder, salt, cornstarch and flour together. Add club soda and stir until blended (batter should be thin). Toss the florets in batter and then place on a wire rack set atop a baking sheet. Allow to sit for about 5 minutes. Working in batches, transfer the cauliflower onto a greased tray in the basket. Cook for 10 to 12 minutes until tender and golden brown.

2. In the meantime, whisk together sesame oil, rice vinegar, vegetable broth, soy sauce, sugar and orange. Add cornstarch and whisk until smooth.

3. Over medium-high heat, heat canola oil in a saucepan. Place in the chiles and then cook while stirring for 1 to 2 minutes until fragrant. Pour in ginger, garlic, orange zest and white part of onions. Cook for 1 minute until fragrant. Add the orange juice mixture and stir. Transfer to saucepan. Heat to boil and then cook while stirring for 2 to 4 minutes.

4. Place the cauliflower into the sauce and then toss to coat. Serve along with rice. Drizzle with thinly chopped green onions.

Nutritional values:

Calories: 528 | Carbohydrates: 97g | Fat: 11g | Saturated Fat: 1g | Sodium: 1614 mg | Fiber: 5g | Protein: 11g

Air-Fryer Chicken Tenders

Preparation Time: 25 minutes | **Cooking Time:** 15 minutes | **Servings:** 4

Ingredients:

- 1 pound chicken tenderloins ½ cup panko bread crumbs 1 tbsp. sour cream
- ¼ cup melted butter
- ½ cup crushed potato sticks 2 tsp fresh chives, minced
- ½ cup cheese crackers, crushed
- 2 bacon strips (cooked & crumbled) ¼ cup Parmesan cheese, grated Extra chives and sour cream

Instructions:

1. Preheat the air fryer to 400 degrees F. Mix the chives, bacon, Parmesan cheese, cheese crackers, potato sticks and bread crumbs in a shallow bowl. Whisk sour cream and butter in a different shallow bowl. Dunk the chicken into the butter mixture and then dip in crumb mixture. Pat to help the coating adhere.

2. Working in batches, spread the chicken on a greased tray in the air fryer basket and drizzle with cooking spray. Air fry for about 7 to 8 minutes on each side until the bird is no longer pink and the coating turns golden brown. Serve with extra chives and sour cream.

Nutritional values:

Calories: 256 | Carbohydrates: 6g | Cholesterol: 84mg | Fat: 14g | Saturated Fat: 7g | Sodium: 267mg | Protein: 29g

Air-Fryer Pork Chops

Preparation Time: 10minutes | **Cooking Time:** 15 minutes | **Servings:** 4

Ingredients:

- Cooking spray Paprika - 1 tsp
- Grated Parmesan cheese - ¼ cup
- Boneless pork loin chops (six ounces each) - 4 Creole seasoning - 1 tsp
- garlic powder - 1 tsp almond flour - 1/3 cup

Instructions:

1. Preheat the air fryer to 375 degrees F. Coat the basket of the air fryer with cooking spray. Combine paprika, Creole seasoning, garlic powder, cheese and almond flour in a shallow bowl. Coat the pork with the flour mixture and shake to get rid of excess. In batches, arrange the pork in the air fryer basket in a single layer and then spray with cooking spray.

2. Air fry for 12 to 15 minutes, flipping when halfway through cooking and drizzling more cooking spray, until golden brown or the internal temperature reaches 145 degrees F. Remove the chops and keep them warm. Repeat with the remaining pork chops.

Nutritional values:

Calories: 310 | Carbohydrates: 4g | Cholesterol: 86mg | Fat: 16g | Saturated Fat: 5g | Sodium: 308mg | Fiber: 1g | Protein: 36g

Air Fryer Nacho Hot Dogs

Preparation Time: 20minutes | **Cooking Time:** 15 minutes | **Servings:** 6

Ingredients:

- 1 cup nacho-flavored tortilla chips, crushed & divided 6 hot dogs
- Sour cream and guacamole, if desired
- 3 cheddar cheese sticks (halved lengthwise) 3 tbsp. sliced & seeded jalapeno pepper
- ¼ cup salsa
- 1-1/4 cups self-rising flour 1/4 tsp chili powder
- 1 cup plain Greek yogurt

Instructions:

1. Make a slit down the length of the hot dogs without slicing through. Inside each slit, insert halved cheese stick and keep hot dogs aside.

2. Preheat the air fryer to 350 degrees F. Combine together ¼ cup of crushed tortill a chips, jalapenos, chili powder, salsa, yoghurt, and flour in a large bowl to form a dough. Transfer the dough on a surface that is floured lightly. Separate into sixths. Roll the dough to form long strips of 15 inches. Wrap 1 strip around the cheese-stuffed hot dog. Repeat this process with the remaining hot dogs and dough. Sprin kle cooking spray onto the dogs and then roll in the remaining crushed chips gentl y. Drizzle cooking spray in the fryer basket and then add the hot dogs in the baske t without touching. This gives room for expansion.

3. Working in batches, air fry for about 8 to 10 minutes until the cheese begins to melt and the dough becomes browned a little. Serve with extra guacamole, sour cre am and salsa if you like.

Nutritional values

Calories: 216 | Carbohydrates: 26g | Cholesterol: 23mg | Fat: 9g | Saturated Fat: 5g | Sodium: 513mg | Fiber: 1g | Protein: 9g | Sugars: 3g

APPETIZERS

Air Fryer Pickles

Preparation Time: 20 minutes | **Cooking Time:** 15 minutes | **Servings:** 5

Ingredients:

- 3 large lightly beaten eggs 32 dill pickle slices
- Ranch salad dressing, if desired 1/2 cup all-purpose flour
- 2 tablespoons fresh dill, snipped 2 cups panko bread crumbs
- 1/2 teaspoon garlic powder 1/2 teaspoon salt
- 1/2 teaspoon cayenne pepper 2 tablespoons dill pickle juice Cooking spray

Instructions:

1. Begin by preheating the air fryer to 400 degrees F. Place the pickles on a paper t owel and let to stand for about 15 minutes until the liquid is almost absorbed.

2. In the meantime, mix the flour and salt in a shallow bowl. Whisk garlic powder, cayenne, pickle juice and eggs in another shallow bowl. In a third bowl, mix the dil l and panko.

3. Dunk the pickles into the flour mixture and coat each side. Shake to remove exc ess flour mixture. Dunk into the egg mixture and then into the crumb mixture and pat so that the coat can adhere. Working in batches, transfer the pickles onto the greased tray in the basket of the air fryer, placing in a single layer. Cook for about 7 to 10 minutes until they are crispy and turned golden brown. Flip the pickles an d drizzle cooking spray on top. Continue to cook for another 7 to 10 minutes until c rispy and golden brown. Serve right away. You can serve with ranch dressing if de sired.

Nutritional values:

Calories: 26 | Carbohydrates: 4g | Cholesterol: 13mg | Fat: 1g | Saturated Fat: 0 | Sodium: 115mg | Fiber: 0 | Protein: 1g

Air Fryer Ravioli

Preparation Time: 20 minutes | **Cooking Time:** 10 minutes | **Servings:** 5

Ingredients:

- 1 cup warmed marinara sauce 1 cup bread crumbs, seasoned Cooking spray
- 1/2 cup all-purpose flour
- 1/4 cup Parmesan cheese (shredded)
- 9 ounces (1 package) frozen beef ravioli, thawed 2 tsp dried basil
- 2 large eggs, beaten lightly Fresh minced basil, if desired

Instructions:

1. Preheat the air fryer to reach a temperature of 350 F. Combine basil, parmesan cheese and bread crumbs in a shallow bowl. Place the eggs and flour in separate shallow bowls. Dunk the ravioli in the flour and coat each side, shaking to remove excess. Immerse in lightly beaten eggs and then dip in the crumb mixture. Pat to help the coating adhere.

2. Working in batches, spread the ravioli on a greased tray in the basket in a single layer. Sprinkle cooking spray on top. Cook ravioli for 3 to 4 minutes until golden brown. Flip and sprinkle cooking spray on top. Continue to cook for another 3 to 4 minutes. You can immediately drizzle basil and some more Parmesan cheese on top if you like. Serve while warm along with marinara sauce.

Nutritional values:

Calories: 40 | Carbohydrates: 6g | Cholesterol: 6mg | Fat: 1g | Sodium: 117mg | Fiber: 1g | Protein: 2g | Sugars: 1g

Bacon-Wrapped Avocado Wedges

Preparation Time: 15 minutes | **Cooking Time:** 10-15 minutes | **Servings:** 2

Ingredients:

- 12 bacon strips
- 2 ripe avocados, medium
- 1 tsp grated lime zest 1-2 tbsp. lime juice
- 2-3 tbsp. Sriracha chili sauce ½ cup mayonnaise

Instructions:

1. Start preheating the air fryer to reach a temperature of 400 F. Slice each avocad o in half. Take out the pit and then peel. Slice each half into thirds. Wrap one slice of bacon around each avocado wedge. In batches of necessary, arrange the wedges in the basket of the air fryer in a single layer and then cook for 10 to 15 minutes u ntil the bacon cooks through.

2. In the meantime, mix together the sriracha sauce, zest, mayonnaise and lime jui ce. Serve the wedges together with the sauce.

Nutritional values:

Calories: 142 | Carbohydrates: 3g | Cholesterol: 9mg | Fat: 13g | Saturated Fat: 3 g | Sodium: 274mg | Fiber: 2g | Protein: 3g | Sugars: 1g

Air Fryer Greek Breadsticks

Preparation Time: 20 minutes | **Cooking Time:** 15 minutes | **Servings:** 6

Ingredients:

- 2 tsp sesame seeds
- 1/4 cup quartered artichoke hearts, marinated and drained If desired, refrige rated tzatziki sauce
- 2 tbsp. pitted Greek olives
- 2 tbsp. Parmesan cheese, grated 1 tbsp. water
- 17.3 ounces (1 package) thawed puff pastry 1 egg, large
- 6 to ½ ounces (1 carton) spreadable spinach and artichoke cream cheese

Instructions:

1. Preheat the air fryer to 325 degrees F. In a food processor, put olives and articho kes. Cover the appliance and then pulse until chopped finely. Take 1 pastry sheet a nd unfold on a surface that is lightly floured. Smear ½ of the cream cheese on top o f half the pastry. Add ½ artichoke mixture on top. Drizzle with ½ of Parmesan che ese. Then fold the plain half over the filling. Seal by pressing gently.

2. Repeat that process with the remaining pastry, parmesan cheese, artichoke mixt ure and cream cheese. Whisk the egg with water. Brush over the tops. Drizzle sesa me seeds on top. Slice each rectangle into 16 strips of ¾ inch wide. Twist the strips a few times.

3. Working batches, spread the bread sticks on a greased tray in the fryer basket i n a single layer. Air fry for 12 to 15 minutes until golden brown. If desired, serve w hile still warm along with tzatziki sauce.

Nutritional values:

Calories: 99 | Carbohydrates: 9g | Cholesterol: 11mg | Fat: 6g | Saturated Fat: 2g | Sodium: 108mg | Fiber: 1g | Protein: 2g

Air Fryer Eggplant Fries

Preparation Time: 15 minutes | **Cooking Time:** 10 minutes | **Servings:** 6

Ingredients:

- 1 cup warmed, meatless pasta sauce 2 eggs, large
- Cooking spray
- ½ cup Parmesan cheese, grated
- 1 medium eggplant (approximately 1-1/4 pounds) ½ cup wheat germ, toasted
- ¾ tsp garlic salt
- 1 tsp Italian seasoning

Instructions:

1. Preheat the air fryer to reach 375 F. Whisk the eggs in a shallow bowl. Combine the seasonings, wheat germ and cheese in a separate shallow bowl.

2. Trim the ends of the eggplant and then slice it lengthwise into half inch slices. Cut the pieces lengthwise into half inch strips. Dunk the strips in eggs and then dip into the cheese mixture to coat.

3. Working in batches, spread the strips on a greased tray in the fryer basket in a single layer. Drizzle cooking spray on top. Air fry for 4 to 5 minutes until golden brown. Flip and then drizzle with cooking spray. Continue to cook for 4 to 5 minutes until golden brown. Serve right away with pasta sauce.

Nutritional values:

Calories: 135 | Carbohydrates: 15g | Cholesterol: 68mg | Fat: 5g | Saturated Fat: 2g | Sodium: 577mg | Fiber: 4g | Protein: 9g | Sugars: 6g

Air Fryer Turkey Croquettes

Preparation Time: 20 minutes | **Cooking Time:** 10 minutes | **Servings:** 6

Ingredients:

- 1-1/4 cups panko bread crumbs
- 2 cups mashed potatoes (with added butter and milk) 2 tbsp. water
- 1/2 cup Parmesan cheese, grated 1 large egg
- 1/2 cup Swiss cheese, shredded
- 3 cups cooked turkey (finely chopped)
- 1/4 tsp dried sage leaves or 1 tsp minced fresh sage 1 finely chopped shallot
- 1/4 tsp pepper 1/2 tsp salt
- 1/2 tsp dried & crushed rosemary or 2 tsp minced fresh rosemary Sour cream, if desired
- Cooking spray (Butter-flavored)

Instructions:

1. Preheat the air fryer to 350 degrees F. Mix sage, rosemary, pepper, salt, shallot, cheeses and mashed potatoes in a large bowl. Add turkey and stir. Shape into 12 patties, one inch thick.

2. Whisk the egg with water in a shallow bowl. In another shallow bowl, add bread crumbs. Dip the croquettes into the egg mixture and then dip in the bowl with bread crumbs. Pat to help coating adhere.

3. Working in batches, put the croquettes on a greased tray in the fryer basket in a single layer. Drizzle with cooking spray. Air fry for 4 to 5 minutes until golden brown. Flip and drizzle with cooking spray. Continue to cook for 4 to 5 minutes until golden brown. Serve with sour cream if you like.

Nutritional values:

Calories: 322 | Carbohydrates: 22g | Cholesterol: 124mg | Fat: 12g | Saturated Fat: 6g | Sodium: 673mg | Fiber: 2g | Protein: 29g | Sugars: 2g

Air Fryer Beef Wellington Wontons

Preparation Time: 35 | **Cooking Time:** 10minutes | **Servings:** 5

Ingredients:

- 1 cup each fresh shiitake, sliced (baby Portobello and white mushrooms)
- 1/2 pound lean ground beef (90 percent lean)
- 1 tbsp. water 1 tbsp. butter 1 egg, large
- 1 tbsp. olive oil
- 12 ounces (1 package) wonton wrappers 2 minced garlic cloves
- 1/4 tsp pepper
- 1-1/2 tsp sliced shallot 1/2 tsp salt
- 1/4 cup dry red wine Cooking spray
- 1 tbsp. fresh parsley (minced)

Instructions:

1. Preheat the air fryer appliance to 325 degrees F. Over medium heat, cook the beef, breaking into crumbles, in a small skillet for about 4 to 5 minutes until the pink color disappears. Place in a large bowl. Over medium-high heat, heat olive oil and butter in the same skillet. Add shallot and garlic and cook for about a minutes. add mushrooms and wine. Stir. Cook for about 8 to 10 minutes the mushrooms become tender. Transfer to beef. Add pepper, salt and parsley and stir.

2. In the middle of each wonton wrapper, pour two teaspoons of the filling. Mix the egg with water. Moisten the edges of wonton with the egg mixture. Then fold the opposite corners over the filling and seal by pressing.

3. Working in batches, spread the wontons on a greased tray in the fryer basket in a single layer. Drizzle cooking spray on top. Cook for about 4 to 5 minutes browned lightly. Flip and drizzle cooking spray. Continue to cook for 4 to 5 minutes until crisp and golden brown. Serve while still warm.

4. Freeze option: Place unbaked wontons in baking sheets lined with parchment. Cover and put in a freezer until firm. Place the wontons in freezer containers and then return to your freezer. When ready to use, cook the pastries as instructed.

Nutritional values:

Calories: 42 | Carbohydrates: 5g | Cholesterol: 9mg | Fat: 1g | Sodium: 82mg | Protein: 2g

Air Fryer Crispy Sriracha Spring Rolls

Preparation Time: 50 minutes | **Cooking Time:** 10 minutes | **Servings:** 6

Ingredients:

- 3 cups coleslaw mix (approximately 7 ounces) Cooking spray
- 3 chopped green onions 24 spring roll wrappers
- 1 tsp seasoned salt
- 1 tbsp. soy sauce
- 2 tbsp. Sriracha chili sauce 1 tsp sesame oil
- 2 packages softened cream cheese (8 ounces each)
- 1 pound chicken breasts, boneless & skinless

Instructions:

1. Preheat the air fryer to 360 degrees F. Combine sesame oil, soy sauce, green oni ons and coleslaw mix. Let to sit while cooking chicken. Arrange the chicken on a gr eased tray in the basket in a single layer. Cook for about 18 to 20 minutes until th e internal temperature reaches 165 degrees F. Remove the chicken and let to cool a bit. Chop the meat finely and toss with the seasoned salt.

2. Increase the temperature of the air fryer to 400 F. Combine Sriracha chili sauce and cream cheese in a large bowl. Stir in coleslaw mixture and chicken. With one c orner of a spring wrapper pointing at you, pour about two tablespoons of the filling below the middle of the wrapper. (Use a damp paper towel to cover the remaining wrappers until when ready to use them.) Fold the bottom corner over the filling an d then moisten the edges with water. Roll the side corners towards the middle over the filling. Fold up tightly and press the tip to seal. Repeat this process with the r emaining wrappers and filling.

3. Working in batches, place the rolls on a greased tray in basket in a single layer. Sprinkle cooking spray on top. Air fry for about 5 to 6 minutes until browned lightl y. Flip and sprinkle with cooking spray. Cook for 5 to 6 minutes until crisp and gol den brown. Serve with some sweet chili sauce and drizzle green onions if you like.

Nutritional values:

Calories: 127 | Carbohydrates: 10g | Cholesterol: 30mg | Fat: 7g | Saturated Fat: 4g | Sodium: 215mg | Protein: 6g | Sugars: 1g

Air Fryer Pork Schnitzel

Preparation Time: 20 minutes | **Cooking Time:** 10minutes | **Servings:** 4

Ingredients:

- Cooking spray
- 1/4 cup all-purpose flour
- 4 pork sirloin cutlets (four ounces each) 1 tsp seasoned salt
- 1 tsp paprika
- 3/4 cup dry bread crumbs 1/4 tsp pepper
- 2 tbsp. 2 percent milk 1 egg, large

Dill sauce

- 1/4 tsp dill weed
- 1 tbsp. all-purpose flour ½ cup sour cream
- ¾ cup chicken broth

Instructions:

1. Preheat the air fryer to 375 degrees F. Combine flour, pepper, and seasoned salt in a shallow bowl. Whisk the milk and egg in another bowl until blended. Combine paprika and bread crumbs in a third bowl.

2. Using a meat mallet, pound the pork cutlets to ¼ inch thickness. Dunk the pork into the flour mixture and coat each side. Shake to remove excess. Dunk into egg mixture and then dip in the crumb mixture. Pat to help the coating stick.

3. Arrange cutlets on a greased tray in the fryer basket in a single layer. Spray with some cooking spray. Air fry for 4 to 5 minutes until golden brown. Flip and drizzle with cooking spray. Continue to cook for 4 to 5 minutes until golden brown. Transfer to a serving plate and keep them warm.

4. In the meantime, whisk broth and flour in a small saucepan until smooth. Heat to boil and stir continuously. Cook while stirring for about two minutes or until thickened. Adjust the heat to low. Add dill and sour cream. Stir and heat through without boiling. Serve along with pork.

Nutritional values:

Calories: 309 | Carbohydrates: 17g | Cholesterol: 91mg | Fat: 13g | Saturated Fat: 5g | Sodium: 572mg | Fiber: 1g | Protein: 30g | Sugars: 2g

Air Fryer Green Tomato Stacks

Preparation Time: 20 minutes | **Cooking Time:** 15 minutes | **Servings:** 8

Ingredients:

- 8 slices of warmed Canadian bacon ¼ cup mayonnaise, fat-free Cooking spray
- ¼ tsp lime zest, grated
- 2 red tomatoes, medium 2 tbsp. lime juice
- 2 green tomatoes, medium
- ¼ tsp dried thyme or 1 tsp minced fresh thyme 2 large egg whites, beaten lightly
- ¼ tsp salt
- ½ tsp pepper (divided) ¾ cup cornmeal
- ¼ cup all-purpose flour

Instructions:

1. Preheat the air fryer to 375 degrees F. Combine ¼ teaspoon of pepper, thyme, lime zest & juice and mayonnaise. Place in your fridge until serving. Pour the flour in a shallow bowl. In another shallow bowl, add egg whites. Combine the remaining ¼ teaspoon of pepper, salt and cornmeal in a third bowl.

2. Slice each tomato crosswise into four pieces. Coat each slice lightly with flour. Shake to remove excess. Immerse in egg whites and then dip in the cornmeal mixture.

3. Working in batches, transfer the tomatoes onto a greased tray in the basket. Spray with cooking spray. Air fry for 4 to 6 minutes until golden brown. Flip and drizzle cooking spray. Continue to cook for 4 to 6 minutes until golden brown.

4. Pile one slice each red tomato, bacon and green tomato for each serving. Serve along with the sauce.

Nutritional values:

Calories: 114 | Carbohydrates: 18g | Cholesterol: 7mg | Fat: 2g | Sodium: 338mg | Fiber: 2g | Protein: 6g | Sugars: 3g

Air Fryer Mushroom Roll-Ups

Preparation Time: 30 minutes | **Cooking Time:** 10 minutes | **Servings:** 10

Ingredients:

- 2 tbsp. extra virgin olive oil Cooking spray
- 8 ounces large Portobello mushrooms, finely chopped, gills discarded 10 flour tortillas (8 inches)
- 1 tsp dried oregano
- 4 ounces whole-milk ricotta cheese 1 tsp dried thyme
- 8 ounces (1 package) softened cream cheese 1/4 tsp salt
- ½ tsp red pepper flakes, crushed

Instructions:

1. Over medium heat, heat oil in a skillet. Place in the mushrooms and then saute for about 4 minutes. Add pepper flakes, salt, thyme and oregano. Saute for 4 to 6 minutes until the mushrooms turn brown. Let to cool.

2. Mix the cheeses and then fold in the mushrooms. Combine thoroughly. Pour 3 tablespoons of the mushroom mixture at the bottom-center of each tortilla. Tightly roll up and hold in place with toothpicks.

3. Preheat the air fryer appliance to 400 F. Working in batches, arrange the roll-up on a greased tray in the fryer basket. Drizzle cooking spray on top. Air fry for about 9 to 11 minutes until golden brown. Once the roll-ups are cooled, get rid of the toothpicks. Serve along with chutney.

Nutritional values:

Calories: 291 | Carbohydrates: 31g | Cholesterol: 27mg | Fat: 16g | Saturated fat: 7g | Sodium: 380mg | Fiber: 2g | Protein: 8g | Sugars: 2g

DINNER

Air Fryer Crispy Curry Drumsticks

Preparation Time: 35 minutes | **Cooking Time:** 15 minutes | **Servings:** 4

Ingredients:

- Minced fresh cilantro, if desired 1 pound chicken drumstick
- 2 tbsp. olive oil 1/2 tsp onion salt
- 2 tsp curry powder 1/2 tsp garlic powder 3/4 tsp salt, divided

Instructions:

1. Place the chicken in a large bowl and then add plenty of water to cover. Pour in ½ teaspoon of salt and leave it stand for 15 minutes at room temperature. Drain off the water and then pat dry.

2. Preheat the air fryer to reach 375 F. Combine the remaining ¼ teaspoon of salt, garlic powder, onion salt, curry powder and oil in a separate bowl. Place in the chicken and then toss to coat it. Working in batches, arrange the meat on a tray in the air fryer basket in a single layer. Cook for 15 to 17 minutes, flipping when halfway through cooking, until the temperature at the center of the meat reaches 170 to 175 degrees F. Drizzle cilantro on top if desired.

Nutritional values:

Calories: 180 | Carbohydrates: 1g | Cholesterol: 47mg | Fat: 13g | Saturated Fat: 3g | Sodium: 711mg | Fiber: 1g | Protein: 15g

Air Fryer Crumb-Topped Sole

Preparation Time: 10 minutes | **Cooking Time:** 10 minutes | **Servings:** 4

Ingredients:

- Cooking spray
- 3 tbsp. reduced-fat mayonnaise 2 tsp melted butter
- 1 cup of soft bread crumbs
- 3 tbsp. Parmesan cheese (grated and divided) 1 finely chopped green onion
- 4 sole fillets (six ounces each) ½ tsp ground mustard
- ¼ tsp pepper
- 2 tsp mustard seed

Instructions:

1. Preheat the air fryer to a temperature of 375 F. Mix the mustard seeds, pepper, 2 tablespoons of cheese and mayonnaise together. Spread on the fillet tops.

2. Arrange the fillets on a greased tray in the fryer basket in a single layer. Air fry for 3 to 5 minutes until the fish easily flakes with a fork.

3. In the meantime, mix together the remaining 1 tablespoon of cheese, ground mu stard, onion and bread crumbs in a small bowl. Add butter and stir. Spread atop th e fillets and gently pat to help adhere. Sprinkle cooking spray on top. Cook for 2 to 3 minutes until golden brown. If you like, drizzle with some more green onions.

Nutritional values:

Calories: 233 | Carbohydrates: 8g | Cholesterol: 89mg | Fat: 11g | Saturated Fat: 3g | Sodium: 714mg | Fiber: 1g | Protein: 24g | Sugars: 1g

Air Fryer Raspberry Balsamic Smoked Pork Chops

Preparation Time: 15 minutes | **Cooking Time:** 15 minutes | **Servings:** 4

Ingredients:

- 1 tbsp. frozen orange juice concentrate (thawed) 2 eggs, large
- 2 tbsp. raspberry jam, seedless 1/4 cup 2 percent milk
- 2 tbsp. brown sugar
- 1 cup panko bread crumbs ¼ cup all-purpose flour 1/3 cup balsamic vinegar
- 1 cup pecans, finely chopped Cooking spray
- 4 smoked bone-in pork chops, 7-1/2 ounces each

Instructions:

1. Preheat the air fryer to 400 degrees F. Whisk milk and eggs together in a shallow bowl. In a separate shallow bowl combine pecans and bread crumbs.

2. Coat the chops with flour and shake to get rid of the excess. Dunk in egg mixture and then dip in crumb mixture. Pat to help adhere. Working in batches, arrange the chops on a greased tray in the fryer basket in a single layer. Sprinkle cooking spray on top.

3. Air fry for about 12 to 15 minutes, flipping when halfway cook time and spraying with more cooking spray, until the chops turn golden brown and the internal temperature reaches 145 degrees F. In the meantime, transfer the remaining Ingredients into a small saucepan and heat to boil. Cook while stirring for 6 to 8 minutes until thickened slightly. Serve along with pork chops.

Nutritional values:

Calories: 579 | Carbohydrates: 36g | Cholesterol: 106mg | Fat: 36g | Saturated Fat: 10g | Sodium: 1374mg | Fiber: 3g | Protein: 32g | Sugars: 22g

Air Fryer Loaded Pork Burritos

Preparation Time: 35 minutes | **Cooking Time:** 5 minutes | **Servings:** 6

Ingredients:

- Cooking spray
- 1 jalapeno pepper (seeded & chopped) 3/4 cup limeade concentrate, thawed
- 1-1/2 cups sour cream 1 tbsp. olive oil
- 15 ounces (1 can) black beans, rinsed & drained 2 tsp salt (divided)
- 6 warmed flour tortillas (12 inches) 1-1/2 tsp pepper (divided)
- 3 cups Monterey Jack cheese, shredded
- 1-
  1/2 pounds boneless pork loin, sliced into thin strips 1 cup long grain rice, uncooked
- 1 cup plum tomatoes, sliced & seeded 1 small green pepper, sliced
- 1/4 tsp garlic powder 1 small onion, sliced 1 tbsp. lime juice
- 1/4 cup & 1/3 cup of minced fresh cilantro, divided

Instructions:

1. Mix the ½ teaspoon of pepper, 1 teaspoon of salt, oil and limeade concentrate in a large shallow dish. Place in pork. Flip to coat. Cover and chill for at least 20 minutes.

2. For the salsa, combine garlic powder, lime juice, jalapeno,, ¼ cup of cilantro, onion, green pepper, tomatoes, and the remaining pepper and salt. Reserve.

3. In the meantime, cook rice as directed on the package. Add the remaining cilantro and stir. Keep it warm.

4. Drain the pork and get rid of the marinade. Preheat the air fryer appliance to a temperature of 350 degrees. Working in batches, arrange the pork on a greased tray in the fryer basket in a single layer. Drizzle cooking spray on top. Air fry for 8 to 10 minutes, flipping halfway cook time, until the pink color of pork disappears.

5. Drizzle 1/3 cup of the cheese off-
center on every tortilla. Lay onto each with half cup of rice mixture, ¼ cup of salsa, ¼ cup of black beans and ¼ cup of sour cream. Add approximately half cup of pork on top. Fold the sides and ends over the filling. Lastly, serve with the remaining salsa.

Nutritional values:

Calories: 910 | Carbohydrates: 82g | Cholesterol: 119mg | Fat: 42g | Saturated F at: 22g | Sodium: 1768mg | Fiber: 9g | Protein: 50g Sugars: 11g

Air Fryer Ham And Cheese Turnovers

Preparation Time: 20 minutes | **Cooking Time:** 10 minutes | **Servings:** 4

Ingredients:

- 2 tbsp. blue cheese, crumbled
- 13.8 ounces (1 tube) chilled pizza crust 1 medium pear, thinly sliced & divided ¼ cup walnuts, chopped & toasted
- ¼ pound black forest deli ham, thinly sliced

Instructions:

1. Preheat the air fryer appliance to 400 degrees F. Unroll the pizza crust in a square of 12-

in. in a lightly floured surface. Slice into four squares. Lay the ham, ½ of pear pieces, walnuts and crumbled cheese diagonally on top of ½ of each square to within half inch of edges. Then fold one corner over the filling to opposite corner, creating a triangle. Seal by pressing the edges with a fork.

2. Working in batches, spread turnovers on a greased tray in the fryer basket. Spray cooking spray on top. Air fry for 4 to 6 minutes per side until golden brown. Top with the remaining pear slices.

Nutritional values:

Calories: 357 | Carbohydrates: 55g | Cholesterol: 16mg | Fat: 10g | Saturated Fat : 2g | Sodium: 885mg | Fiber: 3g | Protein: 15g | Sugars: 11g

Air Fryer Sweet And Sour Pineapple Pork

Preparation Time: 25 minutes | **Cooking Time:** 15 minutes | **Servings:** 4

Ingredients:

- 2 pork tenderloins (each 3/4 pounds), cut in half
- 8 ounces (1 can) pineapple, unsweetened, crushed & undrained Chopped green onions, if desired
- 1 cup cider vinegar ¼ tsp pepper
- ½ cup sugar ¼ tsp salt
- ½ cup dark brown sugar, packed 1 tsp garlic powder
- ½ cup ketchup
- 1 tbsp. Dijon mustard
- 2 tbsp. reduced-sodium soy sauce

Instructions:

1. Mix together the garlic powder, Dijon mustard, soy sauce, ketchup, brown sugar, sugar, cider vinegar and pineapple in a large saucepan. Heat to boil and decrease the heat. Let to simmer while uncovered for 15 to 20 minutes, stirring often, until thickened.

2. Preheat the air fryer to a temperature of 350 degrees. Season the pork with pepper and salt. Arrange the pork on a greased tray in the fryer basket. Air fry for 7 to 8 minutes until pork starts to brown around the edges. Flip and pour ¼ cup of the sauce on top of pork. Continue to cook for about 10 to 12 minutes until the internal temperature reaches 145 degrees. Allow the pork to sit for five minutes prior to slicing. Serve together with the remaining sauce. If you like, add chopped green onions on top.

Nutritional values:

Calories: 489 | Carbohydrates: 71g | Cholesterol: 95mg | Fat: 6g | Saturated Fat: 2g | Sodium: 985mg | Fiber: 1g | Protein: 35g | Sugars: 68g

Spicy Air Fryer Chicken Breasts

Preparation Time: 25 minutes | **Cooking Time:** 20 minutes | **Servings:** 8

Ingredients:

- 1 cup cornmeal
- 2 cups buttermilk
- ¼ tsp dried parsley flakes 2 tbsp. Dijon mustard
- ¼ tsp dried oregano 2 tsp salt
- ½ tsp cayenne pepper 2 tsp hot pepper sauce ½ tsp paprika
- 2 tbsp. canola oil
- 1-1/2 tsp garlic powder ½ tsp ground mustard
- 8 bone-
  in chicken breast halves, without skin (8 ounces each) ½ tsp poultry seasoni
  ng
- 2 cups soft bread crumbs

Instructions:

1. Preheat the air fryer to 375 degrees. Mix the garlic powder, hot pepper sauce, salt, Dijon mustard and buttermilk in a large bowl. Place in chicken and flip to coat. Chill while covered for an hour or overnight.

2. Drain the chicken breasts and get rid of marinade. In a shallow dish, combine together the parsley, oregano, cayenne pepper, paprika, mustard, poultry seasoning, canola oil, cornmeal and bread crumbs. Place in one breast at a time and flip to coat. Arrange on a greased tray in fryer basket in a single layer. Air fry for around 20 minutes, flipping when halfway cook time, until the internal temperature reaches 170 F. Place back all the chicken breasts into the air fryer and cook for 2 to 3 minutes to heat through.

Nutritional values:

Calories: 352 | Carbohydrates: 23g | Cholesterol: 104mg | Fat: 9g | Saturated Fat: 2g | Sodium: 562mg | Fiber: 1g | Protein: 41g | Sugars: 3g

Air Fryer Reuben Calzones

Preparation Time: 15 minutes | **Cooking Time:** 10 minutes | **Servings:** 4

Ingredients:

- 13.8 ounces (1 tube) refrigerated pizza crust
- ½ pound corned beef, sliced & cooked
- 1 cup sauerkraut (rinsed & well drained)
- 4 slices Swiss cheese

Instructions:

1. Start by preheating the air fryer to a temperature of 400 degrees. Unroll the pizza crust dough on a surface that is floured lightly. Pat into a twelve inch square. Slice into four squares. Place one cheese slice, a quarter of sauerkraut and corned beef diagonally atop ½ of each square within half inch of edges. Then fold one corner over the filling to opposite corner, shaping into a triangle. Seal by pressing the edges with fork. Arrange two calzones on a greased tray in your fryer basket in a single layer.

2. Air fry for about 8 to 12 minutes, turning when halfway cook time, until golden brown. Serve along with salad dressing.

Nutritional values:

Calories: 430 | Carbohydrates: 49g | Cholesterol: 66mg | Fat: 17g | Saturated Fat : 6g | Sodium: 1471mg | Fiber: 2g | Protein: 21g | Sugars: 7g

Air Fryer Nashville Hot Chicken

Preparation Time: 30 minutes | **Cooking Time:** 10 minutes | **Servings:** 6

Ingredients:

- Dill pickle slices
- 2 tbsp. dill pickle juice, divided ½ tsp garlic powder
- 2 tbsp. hot pepper sauce, divided 1 tsp chili powder
- 1 tsp salt, divided 1 tsp paprika
- 2 pounds chicken tenderloins 2 tbsp. dark brown sugar
- 1 cup all-purpose flour 2 tbsp. cayenne pepper ½ tsp pepper
- ½ cup olive oil 1 large egg Cooking spray
- ½ cup buttermilk

Instructions:

1. Mix 1 tablespoon of hot sauce, ½ teaspoon of salt and ½ tablespoon of pickle juice in a bowl. Place in chicken and flip to coat. Chill while covered for at least one hour. Drain and discard the marinade.

2. Preheat the air fryer to 375 degrees F. Combine flour, the pepper and remaining ½ teaspoon of salt in a shallow bowl. Whisk buttermilk, egg, and the remaining 1 tablespoon of hot sauce and 1 tablespoon of pickle juice. Dunk the chicken in flour and coat both sides. Shake to remove excess. Dunk in the egg mixture and then dip again in the flour mixture.

3. Working in batches, spread the chicken on a well-greased tray in the fryer basket in a single layer. Spray cooking spray on top. Cook for 5 to 6 minutes until golden brown. Flip and drizzle with cooking spray. Continue to cook for 5 to 6 minutes until golden brown.

4. Whisk together seasonings, brown sugar, cayenne pepper and oil. Add on top of hot chicken and then toss to coat. Serve along with pickles.

Nutritional values:

Calories: 413 | Carbohydrates: 20g | Cholesterol: 96mg | Fat: 21g | Saturated Fat: 3g | Sodium: 170mg | Fiber: 1g | Protein: 39g | Sugars: 5g

Air-Fryer Crispy Curry Drumsticks

Preparation Time: 35 minutes | **Cooking Time:** 15 minutes | **Servings:** 4

Ingredients:

- 1/2 tsp garlic powder 3/4 tsp salt, divided ½ tsp onion salt
- 2 tsp curry powder 2 tbsp. olive oil

Instructions:

1. Put chicken in a large bowl and add plenty of water to cover. Pour in ½ teaspoon of salt. Allow to sit for 15 minutes at lukewarm. Drain off water and pat dry.

2. Preheat the air fryer to 375 degrees F. Combine garlic powder, remaining ¼ teaspoon of salt, onion salt, curry powder, and oil in another bowl. Place in the chicken and toss to coat. Working in batches, arrange the chicken on the tray in the basket in a single layer. Cook for about 15 to 17 minutes, flipping when halfway through cooking, until the internal temperature reaches 170 to 175 F. drizzle with cilantro if desired.

Nutritional values:

Calories: 180 | Carbohydrates: 1g | Cholesterol: 47mg | Fat: 13g | Saturated Fat: 3g | Sodium: 711mg | Fiber: 1g | Protein: 15g

SEAFOOD
Air Fryer Fish And Fries

Preparation Time: 15 minutes | **Cooking Time:** 25 minutes | **Servings:** 4

Ingredients:

- Salt - 1/4 teaspoon salt Pepper - 1/4 teaspoon Olive oil - 2 tablespoons
- 1 pound potatoes, approximate 2 medium

Fish

- Crushed cornflakes - 2/3 cup All-purpose flour - 1/3 cup Egg - 1 (large)
- Pepper - 1/4 teaspoon Water - 2 tablespoons
- Cayenne pepper - 1/8 teaspoon Parmesan cheese - 1 tablespoon (grated) Salt - 1/4 teaspoon
- Tartar sauce, if desired
- Cod fillets or haddock - 1 pound

Instructions:

1. Preheat the air fryer to 400 degrees F. Peel the potatoes and the slice lengthwise into half inch thick pieces. Then chop the slices into half inch thick sticks.

2. Toss the potato sticks with oil, salt, and pepper in a large bowl. Working in batches, put the slices onto the tray in the basket in a single layer. Cook for approximate 5 to 10 minutes until they are just tender. Toss the potato slices to redistribute. Continue cooking for another 5 to 10 minutes until crisp and turned browned lightly.

3. In the meantime, combine the pepper and flour in a shallow bowl. Whisk the egg with water in a separate shallow bowl. Toss the cheese, cayenne and cornflakes together in a third bowl. Drizzle salt onto the fish. Dunk the fish in the egg mixture and coat each side, shaking to remove the excess. Then dunk into the cornflake mixture and pat so that the coating can adhere.

4. Transfer the fries from the air fryer basket and keep them warm. Put the fish on the tray in the basket in a single layer. Let to cook for about 8 to 10 minutes, flipping when halfway through cook time, until the fish flakes easily with a fork and has turned brown lightly. Be sure not to overcook. Place the fries back into the air fryer basket to heat through. You can serve right away. Also, serve along with tartar sauce if you like.

Nutritional values:

Calories: 312 | Carbohydrates: 35g | Cholesterol: 85mg | Fat: 9g | Saturated Fat: 2g | Sodium: 503mg | Fiber: 1g | Protein: 23g | Sugars: 3g

Air Fryer Crumb-Topped Sole

Preparation Time: 10 minutes | **Cooking Time:** 10 minutes | **Servings:** 4

Ingredients:

- Sole fillets (6 ounces each) - 4 Reduced-fat mayonnaise - 3 tbsp. Cooking spray
- Grated Parmesan cheese (divided) - 3 tbsp. Butter (melted) - 2 tsp
- Ground mustard - 1/2 tsp Mustard seed - 2 tsp
- Green onion (finely chopped) - 1 Pepper - 1/4 tsp
- Soft bread crumbs - 1 cup

Instructions:

1. Start by preheating your air fryer to 375 degrees F. Mix two tablespoons of chee se, pepper, mayonnaise and mustard seed. Spread the mixture atop the fillets.

2. Put the fillets on a greased tray in the basket of air fryer in a single layer. Cook the fish for 3 to 5 minutes until it easily flakes with a fork.

3. In the meantime, combine the remaining one tablespoon of cheese, ground must ard, onion, and breadcrumbs in a small bowl. Add butter and stir. Pour spoonfuls o nto the fillets and gently pat to adhere. Sprinkle the topping with cooking spray. C ontinue to cook for 2 to 3 minutes until golden brown. Drizzle some more green oni ons if you like.

Nutritional values:

Calories: 233 | Carbohydrates: 8g | Cholesterol: 89mg | Fat: 11g | Saturated Fat: 3g | Sodium: 714mg | Fiber: 1g | Protein: 24g | Sugars: 1g

Air Fryer Shrimp Po'boys

Preparation Time: 35 minutes | **Cooking Time:** 10 minutes | **Servings:** 4

Ingredients:

- 1/8 tsp cayenne pepper 1/2 cup mayonnaise
- 1-1/2 tsp lemon juice
- 1 tbsp. Creole mustard 1 tbsp. shallot (minced)
- 1 tbsp. chopped dill pickles or cornichons

Coconut shrimp

- 1 medium tomato, thinly sliced 1 cup all-purpose flour
- 2 cups lettuce, shredded 1 tsp herbes de Provence 4 hoagie buns (split)
- 1/2 tsp sea salt Cooking spray 1/2 cup 2% milk
- 1/2 tsp garlic powder
- 2 cups shredded coconut (sweetened) 1/2 tsp pepper
- 1 egg (large)
- 1/4 tsp cayenne pepper 1 tsp hot pepper sauce
- 1 pound shrimp (uncooked) (26 to 30 per pound), peeled and deveined

Instructions:

1. For the remoulade, mix together the mayonnaise, cayenne pepper, lemon juice, dill pickles or cornichons, and shallot in a small bowl. Place in the fridge while covered until serving.

2. Preheat your air fryer to reach 375 F. Combine together cayenne, pepper, garlic powder, sea salt, herbes de Provence and flour in a shallow bowl. Whisk the egg, hot pepper sauce and milk in another shallow bowl. In a third bowl, put the coconut. Dunk the seafood in the flour and coat each side, shaking to remove excess. Then dunk in the egg mixture followed by dipping in the coconut. Be sure to pat to help adhere.

3. Working in batches, spread the shrimp on a greased tray in the basket in a single layer. Sprinkle cooking spray on top. Cook the contents for 3 to 4 minutes each side until the seafood turns pink and the coconut becomes browned lightly.

4. Spread remoulade on the cut side of the buns. Then place shrimp, tomato and lettuce on top.

Nutritional values:

Calories: 716 | Carbohydrates: 60g | Cholesterol: 173mg | Fat: 40g | Saturated F
at: 16g | Sodium: 944mg | Fiber: 4g | Protein: 31g | Sugars: 23g

Air Fryer Wasabi Crab Cakes

Preparation Time: 20 minutes | **Cooking Time:** 10 minutes | **Servings:** 2

Ingredients:

- 1-1/2 cups drained lump crabmeat
- 1 finely chopped sweet red pepper, medium 1/3 cup and 1/2 cup dry bread cr
  umbs, divided 1 finely chopped celery rib
- Cooking spray
- 3 finely chopped green onions, 1/4 tsp salt
- 3 tbsp. reduced-fat mayonnaise 2 egg whites, large
- 1/4 tsp prepared wasabi
- 1/4 tsp celery salt
- 1 sliced green onion
- 1/2 tsp prepared wasabi 1 sliced celery rib
- 1 tbsp. sweet pickle relish
- 1/3 cup reduced-fat mayonnaise

Instructions:

1. Preheat the air fryer to reach 375 F. Combine the sweet red pepper, green onion
s, salt, ¼ tsp prepared wasabi, reduced-
fat mayonnaise, egg whites and 1 finely chopped celery rib. Pour in 1/3 cup of brea
dcrumbs. Then add the crab and fold gently.

2. In a shallow bowl, add the remaining breadcrumbs. Pour heaping tablespoons of
the crab mixture into the breadcrumbs. Coat gently and then form into ¾ inch thic
k patties. Working in batches, spread the crab cakes on a greased tray in the baske
t in a single layer. Sprinkle cooking spray over the cakes. Cook for 8 to 12 minutes,
 gently flipping when halfway cook time and drizzling some more cooking spray, un
til golden brown.

3. In the meantime, add the sauce Ingredients into a food processor and then blend 2
or 3 times or until you achieve the consistency desired. Serve the crab right away a
long with dipping sauce.

__Nutritional values:__

Calories: 49 | Carbohydrates: 4g | Cholesterol: 13mg | Fat: 2g | Sodium: 179mg |
Protein: 3g | Sugars: 1g

Air Fryer Salmon with Maple-Dijon Glaze

Preparation Time: 10 minutes | **Cooking Time:** 15 minutes | **Servings:** 4

Ingredients:

- Butter - 3 tbsp. Maple syrup - 3 tbsp.
- Dijon mustard - 1 tbsp. Medium lemon (juiced) - 1 Minced garlic clove - 1 Olive oil - 1 tbsp.
- Salt - 1/4 tsp Pepper - 1/4 tsp
- Salmon fillets (4 ounces each) - 4

Instructions:

1. Preheat the air fryer until it reaches 400 degrees F. In the meantime, heat the butter in a small saucepan over medium-high heat. Add minced garlic, lemon juice, mustard and maple syrup. Lower the heat and let to simmer for 2-3 minutes until the mixture becomes slightly thick. Transfer from the heat source and reserve.

2. Sprinkle the salmon with olive oil and then season with pepper and salt.

3. Place the seafood in the air fryer basket in a single layer. Allow to cook for 5-7 minutes until the fish just begins to flake easily with a fork and lightly browned. Spritz some sauce on top before serving.

Nutritional values:

Calories: 329 | Carbohydrates: 11g | Cholesterol: 80mg | Fat: 23g | Saturated Fat : 8g | Sodium: 365mg | Protein: 19g | Sugars: 9g

Popcorn Shrimp Tacos With Cabbage Slaw

Preparation Time: 15 minutes | **Cooking Time:** 4-6 minutes | **Servings:** 4

Ingredients:

- 8 warmed corn tortillas, 6 inches 1 tbsp. garlic powder
- 2 cups coleslaw mix
- 1 tbsp. cumin (ground)
- 1/4 cup fresh cilantro, minced
- 1-1/2 cups panko bread crumbs 1/2 cup all-purpose flour
- 2 tbsp. lime juice
- 1 seeded and minced jalapeno pepper, if desired 2 tbsp. honey
- 2 eggs (large) 1/4 tsp salt
- 2 tbsp. 2% milk
- 1 pound peeled and deveined shrimp (41 to 50 per pound), uncooked
- 1 peeled and sliced ripe avocado (medium)
- Cooking spray

Instructions:

1. Mix jalapeno if desired, salt, honey, lime juice, cilantro, and coleslaw mix in a s mall bowl. Toss everything to coat and then reserve.

2. Preheat the air fryer to 375 degrees F. Whisk the milk and eggs in a shallow bo wl. In another shallow bowl, add flour. Combine garlic powder, cumin, and panko i n a third bowl. Dunk the shrimp in flour to coat each side, shaking to get rid of exc ess. Dunk into the egg mixture and then in the panko mixture. Pat to help the coat ing stick.

3. Working in batches, spread shrimp in the air fryer basket that is greased in a si ngle layer. Sprinkle cooking spray on top. Cook the seafood for 2-
3 minutes until golden brown. Flip and sprinkle cooking spray. Continue to cook fo r another 2-3minutes until the shrimp turns pink and golden brown.

4. Lastly, serve the shrimp in tortillas along with avocado and coleslaw mix.

Nutritional values:

Calories: 456 | Carbohydrates: 58g | Cholesterol: 213mg | Fat: 12g | Saturated F at: 2g | Sodium: 414mg | Fiber: 8g | Protein: 29g | Sugars: 11g

Air Fryer Tuna Burgers

Preparation Time: 15 minutes | **Cooking Time:** 5-6 minutes | **Servings:** 4

Ingredients:

- Hamburger buns (split and toasted) -
  4 6.4 ounces (1 pouch) light tuna in water Egg (large and lightly beaten) - 1
- Dry bread crumbs - 1/2 cup Chili sauce - 2 tbsp.
- Celery (finely chopped) - 1/2 cup Onion (finely chopped) -
  1/4 cup Mayonnaise - 1/3 cup
- Sliced tomato and lettuce leaves, if desired

Instructions:

1. Preheat the air fryer until it reaches 350 F. Combine the chili sauce, onion, mayonnaise, celery, bread crumbs and egg in a small bowl. Then fold in the tuna and form into 4 patties.

2. Working in batches, spread the patties on a greased tray in the basket in a single layer. Cook for 5 to 6 minutes on each side until they are browned. Serve atop buns. You can top with tomato and lettuce if you like.

Nutritional values:

Calories: 366 | Carbohydrates: 35g | Cholesterol: 64mg | Fat: 17g | Saturated Fat: 3g | Sodium: 665mg | Fiber: 2g | Protein: 17g | Sugars: 6g

Air Fryer Cod

Preparation Time: 15 minutes | **Cooking Time:** | **Servings:** 2

Ingredients:

- 2 tsp butter
- 1/4 cup fat-free Italian salad dressing 2 cod fillets, 6 ounces each
- 1/2 tsp sugar 1/8 tsp pepper 1/8 tsp paprika
- 1/8 tsp garlic powder 1/8 tsp salt
- 1/8 tsp curry powder

Instructions:

1. Preheat the air fryer to 370 degrees F. Combine the Italian salad dressing, pepper, salt, paprika, curry powder, garlic powder, and sugar in a shallow bowl. Place in the cod and turn to coat it. Set aside to stand for about 10-15 minutes.

2. Arrange the fillets on a greased tray in the basket of your air fryer in a single layer. Discard the rest of the marinade. Cook for about 8 to 10 minutes until the seafood just starts to flake easily using a fork. Add butter on top.

Nutritional values:

Calories: 168 | Carbohydrates: 2g | Cholesterol: 75mg | Fat: 5g | Saturated Fat: 3g | Sodium: 366mg | Protein: 27g | Sugars: 2g

Air Fryer Gingered Honey Salmon

Preparation Time: 10 minutes | **Cooking Time:** 15 minutes | **Servings:** 6

Ingredients:

- Salmon fillet (1-1/2 pounds and 3/4 inch thick) - 1 Honey - 1/4 cup
- Orange juice - 1/3 cup Garlic powder - 1 tsp Ground ginger - 1 tsp
- Reduced-sodium soy sauce - 1/3 cup Green onion (chopped) - 1

Instructions:

1. For the marinade, combine the green, garlic powder, ground ginger, honey, orange juice and reduced-
sodium soy sauce. Mix 2/3 cup of the marinade with salmon. Place in fridge for half an hour and flip frequently. Set aside the remaining marinade for basting.

2. Preheat your air fryer to 325 degrees F. Transfer the fillet onto a greased tray in the basket. Get rid of the remaining marinade. Cook the fish for about 15 to 18 minutes until it just starts to flake with a clean fork. Remember to baste with the reserved marinade during the final 5 minutes.

Nutritional values:

Calories: 237 | Carbohydrates: 15g | Cholesterol: 57mg | Fat: 10g | Saturated Fat : 2g | Sodium: 569mg | Protein: 20g | Sugars: 13g

Air Fryer Pretzel-Crusted Catfish

Preparation Time: 15minutes | **Cooking Time:** 10minutes | **Servings:** 4

Ingredients:

- Lemon slices, if desired
- 4 catfish fillets (six ounces each) Cooking spray
- 1/2 tsp salt
- 4 cups of honey mustard miniature pretzels (coarsely crushed) 1/2 tsp pepper
- 1/2 cup all-purpose flour 2 egg, large
- 2 tbsp. 2 percent milk 1/3 cup Dijon mustard

Instructions:

1. Preheat the air fryer to 325 degrees F. Drizzle the fillets with pepper and salt. In a shallow bowl, whisk the milk, mustard and eggs. Put the pretzels and flour in different shallow bowls. Dip the catfish in flour and then in the egg mixture. Lastly dip in pretzels to coat.

2. Working batches, arrange the fish on a greased tray in the air fryer basket in a single layer. Spray cooking spray on top. Air fry for about 10 to 12 minutes until the fillets easily flake with a fork.

Nutritional values:

Calories: 466 | Carbohydrates: 45g | Cholesterol: 164mg | Fat: 14g | Saturated Fat: 3g | Sodium: 1580mg | Fiber: 2g | Protein: 33g | Sugars: 2g

SIDE DISHES

Air Fryer Garlic-Rosemary Brussels Sprouts

Preparation Time: 5 minutes | **Cooking Time:** 15-18 minutes | **Servings:** 4

Ingredients:

- Fresh rosemary, 1-1/2 teaspoons, minced Panko bread crumbs, ½ cup
- Pepper, ¼ teaspoon Salt, ½ teaspoon
- 2 minced garlic cloves
- Brussels sprouts, 1 pound, trimmed and then halved Olive oil, 3 tablespoons

Instructions:

1. Start by preheating your air fryer to 350 F. Place the garlic cloves, olive oil, pep per and salt into a small microwave-
safe bowl. Heat in a microwave for 30 seconds on high.

2. Mix the Brussels sprouts with two tablespoons of the oil mixture. Put the sprout s into the basket of the air fryer and then cook for about 4 to 5 minutes. Stir the sp routs and then continue to cook for about 8 minutes until they are browned lightly and close to the desired tenderness. Remember to stir when halfway the cooking ti me.

3. Combine the bread crumbs with rosemary and the remaining oil mixture. Drizzl e atop the sprouts. Continue to cook for about 3 to 5 minutes until the sprouts are tender and the crumbs are browned. Serve right away.

Nutritional values:

Calories: 164 | Carbohydrates: 15g | Fat: 11g | Saturated Fat: 1g | Sodium: 342m g | Fiber: 4g | Protein: 5g | Sugars: 3g

Air Fryer Potato Chips

Preparation Time: 30 minutes | **Cooking Time:** 15 minutes | **Servings:** 6

Ingredients:

- 1/2 tsp sea salt
- Cooking spray, olive oil-
  flavored Minced fresh parsley, if desired 2 potatoes, large

Instructions:

1. Preheat the air fryer to 360 degrees F. Chop the potatoes into very thin slices with a vegetable peeler or mandolin. Place on a large bowl. Pour in plenty of ice water to cover. Let to soak for 15 minutes and then drain. Pour in additional ice water and then soak for 15 more minutes.

2. Drain the potatoes and then place them on towels to pat dry. Sprinkle cooking spray atop potatoes and then season with salt. Working in batches, arrange the slices of potatoes on the tray of fryer basket in a single layer. Air fry for 15 to 17 minutes, stirring and flipping every 5 to 7 minutes, until golden brown and crisp. Drizzle with minced parsley if you like.

Nutritional values:

Calories: 148 | Carbohydrates: 32g | Fat: 1g | Sodium: 252mg | Fiber: 4g | Protein: 4g | Sugars: 2g

Air-Fried Radishes

Preparation Time: 15 minutes | **Cooking Time:** 12-15 minutes | **Servings:** 6

Ingredients:

- 1/8 tsp pepper 1/4 tsp salt
- 2-
  1/4 pounds radishes (trimmed & quartered), approximately 6 cups 1 tsp dried oregano or 1 tbsp. minced fresh oregano
- 3 tbsp. olive oil

Instructions:

1. Preheat the air fryer to 375 degrees F. Toss the radishes with the rest of the Ingredients. Transfer the contents onto a greased tray in the fryer basket. Air fry for 12 to 15 minutes while stirring often until crisp-tender.

Nutritional values:

Calories: 88 | Carbohydrates: 6g | Fat: 7g | Saturated Fat: 1g | Sodium: 165mg | Fiber: 3g | Protein: 1g | Sugars: 3g

Garlic-Herb Fried Patty Pan Squash

Preparation Time: 15 minutes | **Cooking Time:** 10 to 15 minutes | **Servings:** 4

Ingredients:

- 1 tbsp. fresh parsley, minced ¼ tsp pepper
- 5 cups halved small patty pan squash (approximately 1-1/4 pounds) ¼ tsp dried thyme
- 1 tbsp. olive oil ½ tsp salt
- ¼ tsp dried oregano
- 2 minced garlic cloves

Instructions:

1. Preheat the air fryer to 375 degrees F. in a large bowl, combine pepper, thyme, oregano, salt, garlic and oil. Sprinkle atop the squash and then toss to coat. Transfer squash onto a greased tray in the basket of your air fryer. Cook for 10 to 15 minutes while stirring often until tender. Drizzle with parsley.

Nutritional values:

Calories: 58 | Carbohydrates: 6g | Fat: 3g | Sodium: 296mg | Fiber: 2g | Protein: 2g | Sugars: 3g

Air Fryer Quinoa Arancini

Preparation Time: 15 minutes | **Cooking Time:** 6 to 8 minutes | **Servings:** 3

Ingredients:

- Warmed pasta sauce, if desired
- 1-3/4 cups cooked quinoa or 9 ounces (1 package) ready-to-serve quinoa 6 cubes part-skim mozzarella cheese (3/4-in each)
- Cooking spray
- 2 large eggs, beaten lightly and divided 1/8 tsp pepper
- 1/2 tsp salt
- 1 tbsp. olive oil
- 1 cup seasoned bread crumbs (divided) 1/2 tsp garlic powder
- 2 tsp dried basil or 2 tbsp. minced fresh basil 1/4 cup Parmesan cheese (shredded)

Instructions:

1. Preheat the air fryer to 375 degrees F. Prepare the quinoa as directed on the package. Add 1 egg, basil, seasonings, oil, Parmesan cheese and ½ cup of bread crumbs.

2. Separate into six portions. Then shape every portion around a cheese cube to form a ball, covering completely.

3. In separate shallow bowls, place the remaining ½ cup of bread crumbs and the remaining egg. Dunk the balls in lightly beaten egg and then roll in the bread crumbs. Transfer onto a greased tray in the fryer basket. Drizzle cooking spray on top. Cook for 6 to 8 minutes until golden brown. Serve along with pasta sauce if desired.

Nutritional values:

Calories: 423 | Carbohydrates: 40g | Cholesterol: 142mg | Fat: 19g | Saturated Fat: 6g | Sodium: 1283mg | Fiber: 5g | Protein: 21g | Sugars: 4g

Air Fryer Roasted Green Beans

Preparation Time: 15 minutes | **Cooking Time:** 20minutes | **Servings:** 6

Ingredients:

- ½ pound mushrooms, fresh & chopped
- 1 pound fresh green beans (chopped into 2 inch slices)
- 1 small red onion (halved & sliced thinly)
- 1/8 tsp pepper ¼ tsp salt
- 1 tsp Italian seasoning 2 tbsp. olive oil

Instructions:

1. Preheat your air fryer appliance to 375 degrees. Mix all the Ingredients and toss to coat.

2. Spread the veggies on a greased tray in the basket. Air fry for about 8 to 10 minutes until they're just tender. Toss to redistribute. Continue to cook for about 8 to 10 minutes until browned.

Nutritional values:

Calories: 76 | Carbohydrates: 8g | Fat: 5g | Saturated Fat: 1g | Sodium: 105mg | Fiber: 3g | Protein: 3g | Sugars: 3g

Air Fryer Herb And Lemon Cauliflower

Preparation Time: 15 minutes | **Cooking Time:** 8 to 10 minutes | **Servings:** 4

Ingredients:

- ¼ tsp red pepper flakes, crushed
- 1 medium head cauliflower, chopped into florets (around 6 cups) ½ tsp salt
- 4 tbsp. olive oil, divided 2 tbsp. lemon juice
- ¼ cup fresh parsley, minced 1 tsp lemon zest, grated
- 1 tbsp. fresh thyme, minced
- 1 tbsp. fresh rosemary, minced

Instructions:

1. Preheat the air fryer to a temperature of 350 F. Combine together 2 tablespoons of olive and cauliflower in a bowl. Toss to coat. Working in batches, spread the cauliflower on a tray in fryer basket in a single layer. Air fry for about 8 to 10 minutes, stirring when halfway cook time, until the florets become tender and the edges turn brown. Mix the remaining Ingredients in a small bowl. Add the remaining two tablespoons of oil and stir. Place the cauliflower in a large bowl. Sprinkle herb mixture on top and then toss to mix.

Nutritional values:

Calories: 161 | Carbohydrates: 8g | Fat: 14g | Saturated Fat: 2g | Sodium: 342mg | Fiber: 3g | Protein: 3g | Sugars: 3g

Breaded Air Fryer Summer Squash

Preparation Time: 15 minutes | **Cooking Time:** 30 minutes | **Servings:** 4

Ingredients:

- ¾ cup Parmesan cheese, grated
- 4 cups thinly chopped yellow summer squash (3 medium) ¾ cup panko bread crumbs
- 3 tbsp. olive oil
- 1/8 tsp cayenne pepper ½ tsp pepper
- ½ tsp salt

Instructions:

1. Preheat the air fryer to 350 degrees F. In a large bowl, add the squash. Pour in s easonings and oil. Mix to coat.

2. Combine cheese and bread crumbs together in a shallow bowl. dunk squash into the crumb mixture and coat each side. Pat to help coating adhere. Working in batc hes, spread the squash on the basket's tray in a single layer. Air fry for about 10 m inutes until the coating is golden brown and squash becomes tender.

Nutritional values:

Calories: 203 | Carbohydrates: 13g | Cholesterol: 11mg | Fat: 14g | Saturated Fat : 3g | Sodium: 554mg | Fiber: 2g | Protein: 6g | Sugars: 4g

Air Fryer Red Potatoes

Preparation Time: 15 minutes | **Cooking Time:** 10 to 12 minutes | **Servings:** 8

Ingredients:

- ¼ tsp pepper
- 2 pounds small unpeeled red potatoes, sliced into wedges ½ tsp salt
- 2 tbsp. olive oil
- 2 minced garlic cloves
- 1 tsp dried & crushed rosemary or 1 tbsp. minced fresh rosemary

Instructions:

1. Preheat the air fryer to 400 degrees F. Sprinkle oil over potatoes. Drizzle with p epper, garlic salt and rosemary. Gently toss to coat.

2. Transfer onto ungreased tray in the basket of your air fryer. Air fry the potatoes for about 10 t0 12 minutes, stirring once, until they're tender and golden brown.

Nutritional values:

Calories: 113 | Carbohydrates: 18g | Fat: 4g | Sodium: 155mg | Fiber: 2g | Protei n: 2g | Sugars: 1g

SNACKS

Air Fryer Mini Nutella Doughnut Holes

Preparation Time: 30 minutes | **Cooking Time:** 5 minutes | **Servings:** 5

Ingredients:

- Confectioners' sugar Nutella - 2/3 cup
- Flaky biscuits (8 count) - 1 tube (16.3 ounces) large and refrigerated Water - 1 tbsp.
- Egg - 1 (large)

Instructions:

1. Preheat the air fryer until it reaches 300 F. Whisk the egg and water together. Roll each biscuit to form a six inch circle on a surface that is lightly floured. Then slice each biscuit into four wedges. Lightly smear the wedges with the egg mixture and then pour 1 teaspoon of Nutella atop of each. Bring up the corners to encase the filling and then seal by pinching the edges firmly.

2. Working in batches, spread the biscuits on ungreased tray in the basket, in a single layer. Cook for 8 to 10 minutes while flipping once until they turn golden brown. Spritz confectioners' sugar on top and then serve while still warm.

Nutritional values:

Calories: 94 | Carbohydrates: 10g | Cholesterol: 6mg | Fat: 6g | Saturated Fat: 1g | Sodium: 119mg | Protein: 1g | Sugars: 4g

Air Fryer Honey Cinnamon Roll-Ups

Preparation Time: 35 minutes | **Cooking Time:** 10 minutes | **Servings:** 24

Ingredients:

- Lemon juice - 1 tablespoon Toasted ground walnuts - 2 cups Water - ½ cup
- Sugar - ¼ cup Sugar - ½ cup
- Ground cinnamon - 2 teaspoons Honey - ½ cup
- Melted butter - ½ cup
- Frozen phyllo dough (thawed) - 12 sheets

Instructions:

1. Preheat the air fryer to 325 degrees. Combine cinnamon, sugar and walnuts.

2. Onto a 15x12-
in. piece of waxed paper, put one sheet of phyllo dough. Rub with butter. Top with another phyllo sheet and brush with butter. (Ensure the remaining dough is well c overed with damp towel to keep it from drying out). Drizzle ¼ cup of walnut mixtu re on top. Tightly roll up jelly-
roll style using waxed paper starting with a long side. Remove the paper as you rol l. Cut the roll into four smaller rolls. Smear with butter and hold in place with toot hpicks. Repeat ¼ cup of walnut mixture and the remaining dough. Working in batc hes, arrange on a greased tray in the basket in a single layer. Air fry for about 9 to 11 minutes until light brown. Place on a wire rack to cool. Get rid of toothpicks.

3. In the meantime, mix all the syrup Ingredients in a small saucepan. Heat to boil a nd let to simmer for about 5 minutes. Allow to cool for ten minutes. Place the rolls on a serving platter. Sprinkle with syrup. Drizzle the remaining walnut mixture on top.

Nutritional values:

Calories: 140 | Carbohydrates: 17g | Cholesterol: 10mg | Fat: 8g | Saturated Fat: 3g | Sodium: 56mg | Fiber: 1g | Protein: 2g | Sugars: 13g

Air Fryer Puff Pastry Danishes

Preparation Time: 25 minutes | **Cooking Time:** 10 minutes | **Servings:** 6

Ingredients:

2/3 cup seedless raspberry jam or jam of choice 8 ounces (1 package) softened cream cheese

17.3 ounces (1 package) frozen puff pastry, thawed ¼ cup sugar

1 tbsp. water

2 tbsp. all-purpose flour 2 egg yolks, large

½ tsp vanilla extract

Instructions:

1. Preheat the air fryer to 325 degrees F. Beat vanilla, flour, sugar, and cream cheese together.

2. Combine the remaining egg yolk with water. Unroll each sheet of puff pastry on a lightly floured surface. Roll to form a 12 inch square. Slice each into 4-in. squares.

3. Pour a tablespoon of cream cheese mixture on each square and then one rounded teaspoon jam. Bring two opposite corners of pastry over the filling. Seal with the yolk mixture. Smear the tops with the remaining yolk mixture.

4. Working in batches, arrange on a greased tray in the basket in a single layer. Air fry for about 8 to 10 minutes until golden brown. Serve while still warm. Place leftovers in a refrigerator.

Nutritional values:

Calories: 197 | Carbohydrates: 20g | Cholesterol: 33mg | Fat: 12g | Saturated Fat: 4g | Sodium: 130mg | Fiber: 2g | Protein: 3g | Sugars: 3g

Air Fryer Herb And Cheese-Stuffed Burgers

Preparation Time: 20 minutes | **Cooking Time:** 15 minutes | **Servings:** 4

Ingredients:

- 4 split hamburger buns
- 2 thinly chopped green onions 2 ounces sliced cheddar cheese 2 tbsp. fresh p arsley, minced
- 1 pound lean ground beef (90 percent lean) 4 tsp Dijon mustard, divided
- ¼ tsp dried sage leaves
- 3 tbsp. dry bread crumbs
- ½ tsp dried & crushed rosemary ½ tsp salt
- 2 tbsp. ketchup

Instructions:

1. Preheat the air fryer appliance to 375 F. Combine 2 teaspoons of mustard, parsl ey and green onions in a small bowl. Combine the remaining 2 teaspoons of mustar d, seasonings, ketchup and bread crumbs in a second bowl. Add beef into the bread crumb mixture. Combine lightly but thoroughly.

2. Form the mixture into 8 thin patties. Put the cheese in the middle of four pattie s. Pour the green onion mixture on top of cheese. Add the remaining patties on top. Firmly press the edge together and ensure you seal completely.

3. Working in batches, put the burgers on a tray in basket in a single layer. Cook f or about 8 minutes. Turn and cook for about 6 to 8 minutes until the internal temp erature reaches 160 F. Serve the burgers atop buns along with your desired toppin gs.

Nutritional values:

Calories: 369 | Carbohydrates: 29g | Cholesterol: 79mg | Fat: 14g | Saturated Fat : 6g | Sodium: 850mg | Fiber: 1g | Protein: 29g | Sugars: 6g

Air Fryer Acorn Squash Slices

Preparation Time: 15 minutes | **Cooking Time:** 15 minutes | **Servings:** 6

Ingredients:

- ½ cup softened butter
- 2/3 cup packed brown sugar 2 medium acorn squash

Instructions:

1. Preheat the air fryer to a temperature of 350 degrees F. Slice the squash in half lengthwise. Remove the seeds and discard. Slice each half crosswise into half inch pieces. Discard the ends. Working in batches, spread the squash on a greased tray in the air fryer basket in a single layer. Cook for 5 minutes on each side until tender.

2. Mix butter and sugar together and then spread on squash. Air fry for 3 more minutes.

Nutritional values:

Calories: 320 | Carbohydrates: 48g | Cholesterol: 41mg | Fat: 16g | Saturated Fat : 10g | Sodium: 135mg | Fiber: 3g | Protein: 2g | Sugars: 29g

Air Fryer Scottish Shortbread

Preparation Time: 15 minutes | **Cooking Time:** 10 minutes | **Servings:** 6

Ingredients:

- 4 to 4-1/2 cups of all-purpose flour 1 cup packed brown sugar
- 2 cups softened butter

Instructions:

1. Preheat the air fryer to 290 degrees F. Cream brown sugar and butter until fluff y and light. Add 3-
3/4 cups of flour. Combine thoroughly. Flip the dough on a floured surface. Knead f or five minutes while adding the remaining flour to make a soft dough.

2. Roll dough to half inch thickness. Then slice into 3x1-
in. strips and prick with fork. Arrange one inch apart on ungreased tray in your fr yer basket. Air fry for 7 to 9 minutes until the cookies set and browned lightly. Let to cool in basket for two minutes. Transfer to wire racks to completely cool.

Nutritional values:

Calories: 123 | Carbohydrates: 12g | Cholesterol: 20mg | Fat: 8g | Saturated Fat: 5g | Sodium: 62mg | Protein: 1g | Sugars: 5g

Air Fryer Bacon Crescent Rolls

Preparation Time: 10 minutes | **Cooking Time:** 10 minutes | **Servings:** 8

Ingredients:

- 1 tsp onion powder
- 6 bacon strips (cooked & crumbled)
- 8 ounces (1 tube) chilled crescent rolls

Instructions:

1. Preheat the air fryer to a temperature of 300 F. Unfold the crescent rolls and divide into 8 triangles. Reserve a tablespoon of bacon. Drizzle the remaining bacon and onion powder onto the triangles. Roll up and drizzle with the remaining bacon. Lightly press to adhere.

2. Working in batches, spread the rolls, in single layer, point side facing downwards, on ungreased tray in basket. Air fry for about 8 to 10 minutes until golden brown. Serve while still warm.

3. Freeze option: Place cooled rolls in freezer containers and then freeze. When ready to use, thaw at room temperature or you can microwave the rolls on high for 10 to 15 seconds until heated through.

Nutritional values:

Calories: 133 | Carbohydrates: 12g | Cholesterol: 6mg | Fat: 7g | Saturated Fat: 1g | Sodium: 322mg | Protein: 4g | Sugars: 3g

Air Fryer Cinnamon Almonds

Preparation Time: 15 minutes | **Cooking Time:** 25 minutes | **Servings:** 2

Ingredients:

- ½ tsp ground cinnamon 1 egg white, large
- 3 tbsp. sugar ½ tsp salt
- 1 tbsp. vanilla extract
- 3 tbsp. packed brown sugar 2 cups unblanched almonds

Instructions:

1. Preheat the air fryer to 300 F. Beat the egg white in a bowl until it becomes frothy. Add vanilla and beat. Pour in almonds and gently stir to coat. Mix the cinnamon, salt and sugars. Transfer to the nut mixture and gently stir to coat.

2. Spread the almonds on a greased tray in the basket in a single layer. Air fry for about 25 to 30 minutes, stirring once, until they're crisp. Let to cool and then store in an airtight container.

Nutritional values:

Calories: 254 | Carbohydrates: 16g | Fat: 19g | Saturated Fat: 1g | Sodium: 163mg | Fiber: 4g | Protein: 8g | Sugars: 11g

Air Fryer Avocado Tacos

Preparation Time: 30 minutes | **Cooking Time:** 10minutes | **Servings:** 4

Ingredients:

- ¼ tsp pepper
- 2 cups coleslaw mix or shredded fresh kale ¼ tsp ground chipotle pepper
- ¼ cup fresh cilantro, minced ¼ tsp salt
- ¼ cup plain Greek yogurt 1 tsp honey
- 2 tbsp. lime juice 1 large beaten egg
- If desired, crumbled queso fresco ¼ cup cornmeal
- 1 medium sliced tomato ½ tsp salt
- 2 medium avocados (peeled & chopped) 8 flour tortillas or corn tortillas (6 in ches)
- ½ tsp garlic powder
- Cooking spray
- ½ tsp ground chipotle pepper

Instructions:

1. In a bowl, mix the Greek yogurt, honey, cilantro, pepper, ¼ teaspoon of chipotle pepper, ¼ teaspoon of salt, lime juice and kale or coleslaw mix. Place in the fridge while covered until serving.

2. Preheat the air fryer appliance to 400 F. in a shallow bowl, add the egg. Combin e together the ½ teaspoon of chipotle pepper, garlic powder, ½ teaspoon salt and co rnmeal. Dunk the slices of avocado in egg and then dip in cornmeal mixture. Pat g ently to adhere.

3. Working in batches, spread slices of avocado on a greased tray in the basket in a single. Drizzle cooking spray on top. Air fry for 4 minutes until golden brown. Flip and drizzle with cooking spray. Cook for another 3 to 4 minutes until golden brow n. Serve the slices in tortillas along with tomato, extra minced cilantro and kale mi x. If desired you can add queso fresco.

Nutritional values:

Calories: 407 | Carbohydrates: 48g | Cholesterol: 39mg | Fat: 21g | Saturated Fat : 5g | Sodium: 738mg | Fiber: 9g | Protein: 9g | Sugars: 4g

DESSERTS
Air Fryer Chocolate Chip Oatmeal Cookies

Preparation Time: 20 minutes | **Cooking Time:** 10 minutes | **Servings:** 6

Ingredients:

- Chopped nuts, 1 cup Softened butter, 1 cup
- Semisweet chocolate chips2 cups Sugar, 3/4 cup
- Salt, 1 teaspoon
- Instant vanilla pudding mix, 3.4 ounces (1 package) 2 large eggs, room temperature
- Brown sugar (packed), 3/4 cup Vanilla extract, 1 teaspoon
- All-purpose flour, 1-1/2 cups Quick-cooking oats, 3 cups Baking soda, 1 teaspoon

Instructions:

1. Preheat the air fryer until it reaches a temperature of 325 F. Cream the sugars and butter for about 5 to 7 minutes until they are fluffy and light. Add vanilla and eggs and beat. In a separate bowl, whisk dry pudding mix, flour, oats, salt and baking soda. Once done, gradually beat the mix into the creamed mixture. Add the nuts and chocolate chips and stir.

2. Pour the dough onto the baking sheets by tablespoonfuls and then flatten a little. Working in batches, place on the greased tray inside the basket of the air fryer one inch apart. Let to cook for about 8 to 10 minutes until they are browned lightly. Transfer onto the wire racks and leave them to cool.

Nutritional values:

Calories: 102 kcal | Carbohydrates: 13g | Cholesterol: 82mg | Fat: 5g | Saturated Fat: 3g | Sodium: 82mg | Fiber: 1g | Protein: 2g | Sugars: 8g

Air Fryer Bread Pudding

Preparation Time: 15 minutes | **Cooking Time:** 15 minutes | **Servings:** 2

Ingredients:

- 4 pieces day-old bread, without crusts and chopped into cubes (approximate 3 cups) 2 ounces chopped semisweet chocolate
- 1/4 tsp salt
- 1 tsp vanilla extract
- 1/2 cup half-and-half cream 1/2 cup 2% milk
- 2/3 cup sugar
- 1 large egg, lukewarm
- Whipped cream and Confectioners' sugar, if desired

Instructions:

1. Heat chocolate in a small microwave-safe bowl until melted. Then stir until smooth. Add cream and stir. Put aside.

2. Whisk vanilla, egg, salt, milk and sugar in a large bowl. Add the chocolate mixture and stir. Add the bread cubes and toss to coat them. Allow to stand for about 15 minutes.

3. Preheat the air fryer to 325 F. Pour spoonfuls of the bread mixture into two 8 oz. ramekins that are greased. Transfer onto the tray of the basket. Cook the contents for 12 to 15 minutes until a knife comes out clean when inserted at the center.

4. Add confectioners' sugar and whipped cream on top if desired.

Nutritional values:

Calories: 729 | Carbohydrates: 107g | Cholesterol: 128mg | Fat: 22g | Saturated Fat: 12g | Sodium: 674mg | Fiber: 2g | Protein: 14g | Sugars: 81g

Air Fryer Caribbean Wontons

Preparation Time: 30 minutes | **Cooking Time:** 10 minutes | **Servings:** 5

Ingredients:

- 24 wonton wrappers
- 1 cup marshmallow creme
- 4 ounces softened cream cheese Cooking spray
- 2 tbsp. chopped walnuts
- 1/4 cup sweetened coconut, shredded
- 2 tbsp. canned pineapple, crushed
- 1/4 cup ripe banana, mashed
- Ground cinnamon and confectioners' sugar
- 1 tsp cornstarch
- ¼ cup sugar
- 1 pound fresh hulled strawberries

Instructions:

1. Preheat the air fryer to a temperature of 350 degrees F. Beat cream cheese in a small bowl until it is smooth. Add pineapple, walnuts, banana and coconut and stir . Then fold in marshmallow crème.

2. Set a wonton paper with one point towards you. Cover the rest of the wrappers with a damp paper towel until when ready to use. Put two teaspoons of the filling i n the middle of the wrapper. Moisten the edges with water. Then fold the opposite corners together to encase the filling and seal by pressing. Repeat this process with the remaining wonton wrappers and filling.

3. Working in batches, place the wontons on a greased tray in the fryer basket in a single layer. Sprinkle with cooking spray. Cook for 10 to 12 minutes until crisp an d golden brown.

4. In the meantime, add the strawberries into a food processor. Cover and then ble nd until the contents are pureed. Mix cornstarch and sugar in a small saucepan. A dd pureed strawberries and stir. Bring to boil and let to cook while stirring for 2 m inutes. Optional, you can strain the mixture, reserve the sauce and get rid of the se eds. Drizzle cinnamon and confectioners' sugar onto wontons. Serve along with sau ce.

Nutritional values:

Calories: 83 | Carbohydrates: 13g | Cholesterol: 5mg | Fat: 3g | Saturated Fat: 1g | Sodium: 67mg | Fiber: 1g | Protein: 1g | Sugars: 7g

Air Fryer Apple Fritters

Preparation Time: 10 minutes | **Cooking Time:** 8 minutes | **Servings:** 15

Ingredients:

- 1 tbsp. 2 percent milk Cooking spray
- 1/4 cup butter
- 1 to 1/2 cups all-purpose flour 1 cup confectioners' sugar
- 1/4 cup sugar
- 2 medium Honeycrisp apples (peeled and sliced) 2 tsp baking powder
- 1 to ½ tsp vanilla extract, divided 2/3 cup 2 percent milk
- 1 tbsp. lemon juice
- 1 to ½ tsp ground cinnamon 2 large eggs, lukewarm
- ½ tsp salt

Instructions:

1. Line parchment onto air fryer basket and cut to fit. Drizzle with cooking spray. Preheat your air fryer to 410 degrees F.

2. Mix cinnamon, baking powder, salt, sugar and flour in a large bowl. Add 1 teaspoon of vanilla extract, eggs, milk and lemon juice. Stir the contents until moistened. Then fold in the apples.

3. Working in batches, pour the dough onto the fryer basket by ¼ cupfuls placing two inch apart. Drizzle with cooking spray. Air fry for 5 to 6 minutes until golden brown. Flip the fritters and continue to cook for 1 to 2 minutes.

4. In a small saucepan, heat butter over medium heat until melted. Gently heat for about 5 minutes until the butter begins to foam and brown. Transfer from the heat source and let to cool a bit. Pour in the remaining ½ teaspoon of vanilla extract, 1 tablespoon of milk and confectioners' sugar. Whisk until smooth. Sprinkle on top of the fritters prior to serving.

Nutritional values:

Calories: 145 | Carbohydrates: 24g | Cholesterol: 34mg | Fat: 4g | Saturated Fat: 2g | Sodium: 183mg | Fiber: 1g | Protein: 3g | Sugars: 14g

Air Fryer Lemon Slice Sugar Cookies

Preparation Time: 15 minutes | **Cooking Time:** 10 minutes | **Servings:** 6

Ingredients:

- 1 large egg, lukewarm
- ½ cup butter, unsalted & softened ¼ tsp salt
- 3.4 ounces (1 package) instant lemon pudding mix 1 tsp baking powder
- ½ cup sugar
- 1-1/2 cups all-purpose flour 2 tbsp. 2 percent milk
- 2-4 tsp lemon juice
- 2/3 cup confectioners' sugar

Instructions:

1. Cream pudding mix, sugar and butter in a large bowl for about 5 to 7 minutes until fluffy and light. Add milk and egg and beat. Whisk baking powder, salt and flour in a separate bowl. Then slowly beat into the creamed mixture.

2. Separate the dough in ½. Shape each half into a long roll of 6 inches on a lightly floured surface. Wrap and chill for about 3 hours until firm.

3. Preheat the air fryer to 325 F. Unwrap the dough and then cut crosswise into half inch slices. Working in batches, arrange the slices on a greased tray in the fryer basket in a single layer. Cook for about 8 to 12 minutes until the edges become light brown. Let to cool for two minutes in the basket. Transfer onto wire racks to cool completely.

4. Combine together confectioners' sugar and sufficient amount of lemon juice until you reach a sprinkling consistency. Spray onto the cookies. Let to sit until set.

5. Making in advance: You can prepare the dough two days before. Wrap and put into a resealable container. Keep in your fridge.

6. Freeze option: Put wrapped logs into a container that is sealable and place in a freezer. When ready to use, unwrap the logs and chop into slices. Cook as instructed but increase the time by 1 to 2 minutes.

Nutritional values:

Calories: 110 | Carbohydrates: 17g | Cholesterol: 18mg | Fat: 4g | Saturated Fat: 2g | Sodium: 99mg | Protein: 1g | Sugars: 11g

Air Fryer Peppermint Lava Cakes

Preparation Time: 15 minutes | **Cooking Time:** 10-15 | **Servings:** 4

Ingredients:

- If desired, 2 tbsp. peppermint candies (finely crushed) 2/3 cup of semisweet c hocolate chips
- 6 tbsp. all-purpose flour ½ cup cubed butter
- 1 tsp peppermint extract
- 1 cup of confectioners' sugar 2 large egg yolks, lukewarm 2 large eggs, lukew arm

Instructions:

1. Preheat the air fryer to 375 degrees. Melt butter and chocolate chips for 30 seco nds in a microwave-
safe bowl. Stir until the liquid is smooth. Whisk in egg yolks, extract, eggs and conf ectioners' sugar until blended. Then fold in the flour.

2. Generously coat four 4-
oz ramekins with grease and flour. Transfer the batter into the coated ramekins. D on't overfill. Place the ramekins on the tray of your fryer basket and then cook for about 10 to 15 minutes until the edges of the cake set and the temperature reaches 160 F. Avoid overcooking.

3. Transfer from the basket and let to sit for about 5 minutes. Gently run a clean k nife a few times around the sides of ramekins to loosen the cake. Invert on top of pl ates. Drizzle crushed candies on top. Serve right away.

Nutritional values:

Calories: 563 | Carbohydrates: 57g | Cholesterol: 246mg | Fat: 36g | Saturated F at: 21g | Sodium: 226mg | Fiber: 2g | Protein: 7g | Sugars: 45g

Air Fryer Honeyed Pears In Puff Pastry

Preparation Time: 25 minutes | **Cooking Time:** 15 minutes | **Servings:** 4

Ingredients:

1 large lightly beaten egg 4 small pears

1 sheet frozen puff pastry (thawed) 4 cups of water

1 vanilla bean 2 cups sugar

6-8 whole cloves 1 cup of honey

3 cinnamon sticks (3 inches) 1 small lemon, cut in half

Instructions:

1. Start by coring the pears from bottom and leave the stems intact. Peel and then slice ¼ inch from bottom of each to the level if need be.

2. Mix cloves, cinnamon, lemon halves, honey, sugar and water in a large saucepan . Bust the vanilla bean and then scrape seeds. Place the seeds and bean into the sugar mixture. Heat to boil and then reduce heat. Put the pears on their sides in the saucepan. Poach while uncovered for about 16 to 20 minutes, basting often with poaching liquid, until almost tender.

3. Remove the pears using a slotted spoon and let to cool a bit. Strain and then set aside 1-1/2 cups of poaching liquid. Reserve.

4. Preheat the air fryer to a temperature of 325 F. On a lightly floured surface, unfold the puff pastry. Slice into half inch-
wide strips. Light smear with beaten egg. Starting from the bottom of pear, wrap one pastry strip around the pear while adding more strips until the pear is wrapped completely in pastry. Repeat this process with the remaining puff pastry and pears.

5. Spread the pears on a greased tray in your air fryer basket in a single layer. Air fry for 12 to 15 minutes until golden brown.

6. In the meantime, heat the reserved poaching liquid to boil and cook for about ten minutes until the liquid is syrupy and thick. Transfer the pears on dessert plates and drizzle syrup on top. Serve while still warm.

Nutritional values:

Calories: 536 | Carbohydrates: 92g | Cholesterol: 47mg | Fat: 18g | Saturated Fat : 4g | Sodium: 223mg | Fiber: 9g | Protein: 7g | Sugars: 50g

Air Fryer Mini Chimichangas

Preparation Time: 1 hour | **Cooking Time:** 10 minutes | **Servings:** 14

Ingredients:

- Salsa
- 1-pound ground beef Cooking spray
- 1 medium sliced onion
- 1 large egg white, beaten lightly
- 1 envelope taco seasoning
- 14 egg roll wrappers 3/4 cup water
- 4 ounces (1 can) sliced green chiles, drained
- 1 cup sour cream
- 3 cups Monterey Jack cheese, shredded

Instructions:

1. Over medium heat, cook the onion and beef in a large skillet until the pink color of meat disappears. Crumble the meat and drain. Add in water and taco seasoning and stir. Heat to boil. Reduce the heat. Let to simmer while uncovered for five minutes, stirring often. Transfer from heat and let to cool a bit.

2. Preheat the air fryer to a temperature of 375 F. Mix chiles, sour cream, and cheese in a large bowl. Add the beef mixture and stir. On a work surface, place one egg wrapper with a corner pointing at you. Pour 1/3 cup of the filing in the middle. Fold bottom one-third of the wrapper over the filling. Then fold in the sides.

3. Brush egg white onto top point. Roll up to seal. Repeat this with the remaining filling and wrappers. (Ensure you cover the remaining wrappers with waxed paper to prevent them from drying out.)

4. Working in batches, arrange the chimichangas on a greased tray in the fryer basket in a single layer. Drizzle cooking spray on top. Air fry for 3 to 4 minutes per side until golden brown. Serve while still warm with salsa and extra sour cream.

Nutritional values:

Calories: 294 | Carbohydrates: 23g | Cholesterol: 48mg | Fat: 15g | Saturated Fat : 8g | Sodium: 618mg | Dietary Fiber: 1g | Protein: 16g | Sugars: 1g

Air Fryer Apple Pie Egg Rolls

Preparation Time: 25 minutes | **Cooking Time:** 15 minutes | **Servings:** 8

Ingredients:

2/3 cup of hot caramel ice cream topping

3 cups tart apples, chopped & peeled

1 tbsp. sugar

½ cup packed light brown sugar Cooking spray - Butter-flavored

8 egg roll wrappers

2-1/2 tsp ground cinnamon, divided

½ cup spreadable cream cheese

1 tsp cornstarch

Instructions:

1. Preheat the air fryer appliance to a temperature of 400 F. Combine together cornstarch, two teaspoons of cinnamon, brown sugar and apples in a small bowl. With one corner of an egg wrapper pointing at you, pour one scant tablespoon of cream cheese to within one inch of edges. Then spread 1/3 cup of the apple mixture beneath the middle of wrapper. (Use a damp paper towel to cover the remaining wrappers until when you're ready to use.)

2. Roll the bottom corner over the filling. Moisten the remaining edges of the wrapper with water. Roll the side corners towards the middle over the filling. Tightly roll up the egg roll and seal by pressing at the tip. Repeat with remaining wrappers.

3. Working in batches, spread the egg rolls on a greased tray in fryer basket in a single layer. Spray with cooking spray. Air fry for 5 to 6 minutes until golden brown. Flip and spray with cooking spray. Cook for another 5 to 6 minutes until crisp and golden brown. Mix the remaining half teaspoon of cinnamon with sugar. Roll the hot egg rolls in the mix. Serve along with caramel sauce.

Nutritional values:

Calories: 273 | Carbohydrates: 56g | Cholesterol: 13mg | Fat: 4g | Saturated Fat: 2g | Sodium: 343mg | Fiber: 2g | Protein: 5g | Sugars: 35g

BONUS

Garlic Shells

Yield: 5 servings | **Prep Time:** 25 minutes | **Cook Time:** 15 minutes

Ingredients:

- 10 oz jumbo shells pasta, cooked
- 1 cup marinara sauce
- 5 oz firm tofu, crumbled
- 1 teaspoon garlic powder
- ½ cup spinach, grinded
- 1 tablespoon olive oil

Instructions:

1. In the mixing bowl, mix up, olive oil, crumbled tofu, garlic powder, and spinach.

2. Then fill the jumbo shells pasta with garlic mixture.

3. Put the stuffed shells pasta in the casserole mold and top with marinara sauce.

4. Cover the mold with foil and bake in the preheated to 365F oven for 15 minutes.

Per Serving: 303 calories,10.5g protein, 49.4g carbohydrates, 6.4g fat, 3.7g fiber, 1 mg cholesterol, 211mg sodium, 329mg potassium.

Seitan Patties

Yield: 3 servings | **Prep Time:** 10 minutes | **Cook Time:** 25 minutes

Ingredients:

- ¼ onion, diced
- 1 bell pepper, chopped
- 8 oz seitan chunks
- 1 teaspoon coconut oil
- 1 teaspoon ground cumin
- ¼ cup oatmeal
- 1 oz walnuts, chopped
- ¼ teaspoon cayenne pepper

Instructions:

1. Blend together onion, bell pepper, seitan chunks, coconut oil, ground cumin, oat meal, walnuts, and cayenne pepper.

2. When the mixture is smooth, transfer it in the bowl. 3. Preheat the oven to 365F
.

4. Make 3 patties and transfer them in the lined baking tray. 5. Bake the patties for 25 minutes at 360F until they are light

brown and a little bit crispy.

Per Serving: 522 calories,60.1g protein, 31.1g carbohydrates, 18.2g fat, 2.2g fiber, 0mg cholesterol, 3mg sodium, 178mg potassium.

Sweet & Sour Brussel Sprouts

Yield: 2 servings | **Prep Time:** 10 minutes | **Cook Time:** 17 minutes

Ingredients:

- 1 cup Brussel sprouts, sliced
- 1 teaspoon liquid honey
- 1 teaspoon white pepper
- 3 tablespoons soy sauce, low-sodium
- 1 tablespoon olive oil
- 1 tablespoon pumpkin seeds, chopped

Instructions:

1. Heat up olive oil in the skillet.

2. Add sliced Brussel sprouts and roast them for 10 minutes. Stir the vegetables oc casionally.

3. After this, sprinkle them with white pepper, soy sauce, and liquid honey. Stir th e vegetables well and cook for 3 minutes.

4. Add pumpkin seeds and mix up well. 5. Cook the meal for 2 minutes more.

Per Serving: 109 calories,5.3g protein, 7.7g carbohydrates, 7.3g fat, 1.9g fiber, 12 mg cholesterol, 134mg sodium, 250mg potassium.

Baked Tempeh

Yield: 6 servings | **Prep Time:** 10 minutes | **Cook Time:** 14 minutes

Ingredients:

- 1-pound tempeh, cubed
- ¼ cup low-sodium tamari
- 1 teaspoon nutritional yeast

Instructions:

1. Mix up tamari and nutritional yeast.

2. Then dip the tempeh cubes in the liquid and transfer in the lined with a baking paper baking tray.

3. Bake the tempeh for 14 minutes at 385F. Flip the tempeh cubes on another side after 7 minutes of cooking.

Per Serving: 154 calories,14.8g protein, 8.3g carbohydrates, 8.2g fat, 0.2g fiber, 0 mg cholesterol, 361mg sodium, 344mg potassium.

Marinated Tofu

Yield: 3 servings | **Prep Time:** 20 minutes | **Cook Time:** 8 minutes

Ingredients:

- 10 oz firm tofu, cubed
- 1 tablespoon olive oil
- 1 tablespoon rice vinegar
- 1 teaspoon Italian seasonings
- 1 tablespoon marinara sauce
- 1 teaspoon coconut oil
- ½ teaspoon chili flakes

Instructions:

1. Make the marinade: mix up olive oil, rice vinegar, Italian seasonings, and marinara sauce. Add chili flakes and whisk the mixture gently.

2. Then sprinkle the tofu cubes with the marinade and leave for 10-15 minutes in the fridge.

3. Meanwhile, heat up coconut oil in the skillet.

4. Put the marinated tofu in the skillet in one layer and roast for 2 minutes per side or until the tofu cubes are light brown.

Per Serving: 132 calories, 7.8g protein, 2.5g carbohydrates, 10.7g fat, 1g fiber, 1mg cholesterol, 33mg sodium, 158mg potassium.

Zucchanoush

Yield: 6 servings | **Prep Time:** 10 minutes | **Cook Time:** 35 minutes

Ingredients:

- 4 zucchinis, chopped
- 2 tablespoons olive oil
- 1 teaspoon harissa
- 1 tablespoon tahini paste
- 1 teaspoon pine nuts, roasted
- ¼ teaspoon garlic powder
- ½ teaspoon dried mint

Instructions:

1. Preheat the oven to 365F.

2. Put the zucchinis in the baking tray, sprinkle with olive oil and bake in the oven for 35 minutes or until the vegetables are tender.

3. Then transfer the zucchinis in the food processor.

4. Add harissa, tahini paste, pine nuts, garlic powder, and dried mint.

5. Blend the meal until smooth.

Per Serving: 123 calories,3.2g protein, 8.1g carbohydrates, 10.1g fat, 2.6g fiber, 0 mg cholesterol, 39mg sodium, 536mg potassium.

Garden Stuffed Squash

Yield: 2 servings | **Prep Time:** 15 minutes | **Cook Time:** 45 minutes

Ingredients:

- 12 oz butternut squash, halved
- 1 bell pepper, chopped
- 5 oz leek, chopped
- 1 teaspoon dried sage
- 1 tablespoon coconut oil
- 2 oz vegan mozzarella, shredded

Instructions:

1. Melt the coconut oil in the skillet.

2. Add bell pepper and leek. Roast the vegetables for 3 minutes. 3. After this, add dried sage and stir well.

4. Fill the butternut squash with the vegetable's mixture and top with vegan Mozzarella.

5. Bake the squash halves at 360F for 40 minutes.

Per Serving: 289 calories, 4.4g protein, 41.6g carbohydrates, 13.4g fat, 5.6g fiber, 0 mg cholesterol, 233mg sodium, 842mg potassium.

Broccoli Balls

Yield: 4 servings | **Prep Time:** 15 minutes | **Cook Time:** 10 minutes

Ingredients:

- 1 cup broccoli, shredded
- ¼ cup quinoa, cooked
- 1 teaspoon nutritional yeast
- ½ teaspoon ground coriander
- 1 tablespoon flax meal
- 1 egg, beaten
- 2 tablespoons avocado oil

Instructions:

1. Mix up broccoli, quinoa, nutritional yeast, ground coriander, flax meal, and egg.

2. Stir the mixture until homogenous. 3. Then make the medium size balls. 4. Heat up avocado oil for 1 minute.

5. Put the broccoli balls in the hot avocado oil and cook them for 2 minutes per side or until light brown.

Per Serving: 82 calories,4.4g protein, 9.7g carbohydrates, 3.4g fat, 2.4g fiber, 41mg cholesterol, 24mg sodium, 203mg potassium.

Vegetarian Sloppy Joes

Yield: 2 servings | **Prep Time:** 15 minutes | **Cook Time:** 45 minutes

Ingredients:

- ½ cup green lentils
- 1 white onion, diced
- 1 teaspoon chili pepper
- ½ teaspoon smoked paprika
- 2 tablespoons tomato paste
- 1 tablespoon sesame oil
- 1 teaspoon liquid honey
- 2 cups of water
- ½ cup of coconut milk

Instructions:

1. Pour sesame oil in the saucepan.

2. Add white onion, chili pepper, smoked paprika, and cook the ingredients for 4 minutes.

3. Then add green lentils, tomato paste, liquid honey, and water. 4. Add coconut milk and stir the mixture well.

5. Close the lid and cook the sloppy joes on medium heat for 40 minutes.

6. Then remove the meal from the heat and leave it for 10 minutes to rest.

Per Serving: 416 calories, 15.2g protein, 43.8g carbohydrates, 21.8g fat, 18.1g fiber, 0mg cholesterol, 38mg sodium, 883mg potassium.

Tofu Stroganoff

Yield: 2 servings | **Prep Time:** 15 minutes | **Cook Time:** 25 minutes

Ingredients:

- 4 oz egg noodles
- 6 oz firm tofu, chopped
- 1 tablespoon whole-wheat flour
- 1 onion, sliced
- 1 tablespoon coconut oil
- 1 teaspoon ground black pepper
- ½ teaspoon smoked paprika
- ½ cup of soy milk
- ½ cup of water

Instructions:

1. Roast the sliced onion with coconut oil in the saucepan until light brown.

2. Then add ground black pepper, smoked paprika, water, and egg noodles.

3. Bring the mixture to boil and cook it for 8 minutes.

4. After this, mix up flour and soy milk and pour the liquid in the stroganoff mixture.

5. Add tofu and carefully mix up the mixture.

6. Close the lid and cook tofu stroganoff for 5 minutes. Leave the cooked meal for 10 minutes to rest.

Per Serving: 270 calories, 12.7g protein, 28.7g carbohydrates, 12.8g fat, 3.6g fiber, 16mg cholesterol, 49mg sodium, 330mg potassium.

Turmeric Cauliflower Florets

Yield: 4 servings | **Prep Time:** 10 minutes | **Cook Time:** 25 minutes

Ingredients:

- 2 cups cauliflower florets
- 1 tablespoon ground turmeric
- 1 teaspoon smoked paprika
- 1 tablespoon olive oil

Instructions:

1. Sprinkle the cauliflower florets with ground turmeric, smoked paprika, and olive oil.

2. Then line the baking tray with baking paper and put the cauliflower florets in the tray in one layer.

3. Bake the meal for 25 minutes at 375F or until the cauliflower florets are tender.

Per Serving: 50 calories,1.2g protein, 4.1g carbohydrates, 3.8g fat, 1.8g fiber, 0mg cholesterol, 16mg sodium, 207mg potassium.

Tempeh Reuben

Yield: 4 servings | **Prep Time:** 25 minutes | **Cook Time:** 10 minutes

Ingredients:

- 10 oz tempeh
- ½ cup low-sodium vegetable broth
- 1 teaspoon apple cider vinegar
- 1 teaspoon garlic powder
- 1 tablespoon olive oil

Instructions:

1. In the bowl mix up the vegetable broth, apple cider vinegar, and garlic powder.

2. Then put tempeh in the liquid and leave it to marinate for 15-20 minutes.

3. After this, cut tempeh into servings and put in the well-preheated skillet.

4. Add olive oil and cook it for 4 minutes per side or until golden brown.

Per Serving: 171 calories, 13.5g protein, 7.3g carbohydrates, 11.2g fat, 0.1g fiber, 0 mg cholesterol, 47mg sodium, 302mg potassium.

Marinated Tofu Skewers

Yield: 4 servings | **Prep Time:** 25 minutes | **Cook Time:** 20 minutes

Ingredients:

- ¼ cup low-fat yogurt
- 1 teaspoon curry powder
- 1 onion, diced
- 1-pound firm tofu, cubed
- ½ teaspoon chili flakes
- 1 teaspoon ground paprika

Instructions:

1. In the mixing bowl mix up yogurt, curry powder, onion, chili flakes, and ground paprika.

2. Then mix up yogurt mixture and cubed tofu. Leave tofu for 20 minutes to marinate.

3. After this, string the tofu cubes on the skewers and place them in the baking tray.

4. Bake the tofu for 12 minutes at 375F or until it is light brown.

Per Serving: 105 calories,10.6g protein, 6.2g carbohydrates, 5.1g fat, 2g fiber, 1mg cholesterol, 26mg sodium, 265mg potassium.

Spinach Casserole

Yield: 3 servings | **Prep Time:** 5 minutes | **Cook Time:** 30 minutes

Ingredients:

- 2 cups spinach, chopped
- 4 oz artichoke hearts, chopped
- ¼ cup low-fat yogurt
- 1 teaspoon Italian seasonings
- 2 oz vegan mozzarella, shredded

Instructions:

1. Mix up all ingredients in the casserole mold and cover it with foil.

2. Then transfer it in the preheated to 365F oven and bake it for 30 minutes.

Per Serving: 102 calories,3.7g protein, 11g carbohydrates, 4.9g fat, 2.5g fiber, 2mg cholesterol, 206mg sodium, 300mg potassium.

Tofu Turkey

Yield: 6 servings | **Prep Time:** 15 minutes | **Cook Time:** 75 minutes

Ingredients:

- 1 onion, diced
- 1 cup mushrooms, chopped
- 1 bell pepper, chopped
- 12 oz firm tofu, crumbled
- 1 teaspoon dried rosemary
- 1 tablespoon avocado oil
- ½ cup marinara sauce
- 1 teaspoon miso paste

Instructions:

1. Saute onion, mushrooms, bell pepper, rosemary, miso paste, and avocado oil in the saucepan until the ingredients are cooked (appx.10-15 minutes).

2. Then put ½ part of tofu in the round baking pan. Press well and make the medium whole in the center.

3. Put the mushroom mixture in the tofu whole and top it with marinara sauce.

4. Add remaining tofu and press it well. Cover the meal with foil. 5. Bake the tofu turkey for 60 minutes at 395F.

Per Serving: 80 calories,5.9g protein, 7.9g carbohydrates, 3.4 fat, 2.1g fiber, 0mg cholesterol, 130mg sodium, 262mg potassium.

Cauliflower Tots

Yield: 4 servings | **Prep Time:** 15 minutes | **Cook Time:** 20 minutes

Ingredients:

- 1 cup cauliflower, shredded
- 3 oz vegan Parmesan, grated
- 1/3 cup flax seeds meal
- 1 egg, beaten
- 1 teaspoon Italian seasonings
- 1 teaspoon olive oil

Instructions:

1. In the bowl mix up shredded cauliflower, vegan Parmesan, flax seeds meal, egg, and Italian seasonings.

2. Knead the cauliflower mixture. Add water if needed.

3. After this, make the cauliflower tots from the mixture.

4. Line the baking tray with baking paper and place the

cauliflower tots inside.

5. Sprinkle them with the olive oil and transfer in the preheated to 375F oven.

6. Bake the meal for 15-20 minutes or until golden brown.

Per Serving: 109 calories, 6.1g protein, 6.3g carbohydrates, 6.6g fat, 3.7g fiber, 42 mg cholesterol, 72mg sodium, 158mg potassium.

Zucchini Soufflé

Yield: 6 servings | **Prep Time:** 10 minutes | **Cook Time:** 60 minutes

Ingredients:

- 2 cups zucchini, grated
- ½ teaspoon baking powder
- ½ cup oatmeal, grinded
- 1 onion, diced
- 3 tablespoons water
- 1 teaspoon cayenne pepper
- 1 teaspoon dried thyme

Instructions:

1. Mix up all ingredients together in the casserole mold. 2. Flatten well the zucchini mixture and cover with foil. 3. Bake the soufflé at 365F for 60 minutes.

Per Serving: 41 calories,1.6g protein, 8.1g carbohydrates, 0.6g fat, 1.6g fiber, 0mg cholesterol, 6mg sodium, 200mg potassium.

Honey Sweet Potato Bake

Yield: 4 servings | **Prep Time:** 20 minutes | **Cook Time:** 20 minutes

Ingredients:

- 4 sweet potatoes, baked
- 1 tablespoon honey
- 1 teaspoon ground cinnamon
- ¼ teaspoon ground cardamom
- 1/3 cup soy milk

Instructions:

1. Peel the sweet potatoes and mash them.

2. Then mix mashed potato with ground cinnamon, cardamom, and soy milk. Stir it well.

3. Transfer the mixture in the baking pan and flatten well.

4. Sprinkle the mixture with honey and cover with foil.

5. Bake the meal at 375F for 20 minutes.

Per Serving: 30 calories, 0.7g protein, 6.5g carbohydrates, 0.4g fat, 0.5g fiber, 0mg cholesterol, 11mg sodium, 39mg potassium.

Lentil Quiche

Yield: 4 servings | **Prep Time:** 15 minutes | **Cook Time:** 35 minutes

Ingredients:

- 1 cup green lentils, boiled
- ½ cup carrot, grated
- 1 onion, diced
- 1 tablespoon olive oil
- ¼ cup flax seeds meal
- 1 teaspoon ground black pepper
- ¼ cup of soy milk

Instructions:

1. Cook the onion with olive oil in the skillet until light brown.

2. Then mix up cooked onion, lentils, and carrot.

3. Add flax seeds meal, ground black pepper, and soy milk. Stir the mixture until homogenous.

4. After this, transfer it in the baking pan and flatten ell.

5. Bake the quiche for 35 minutes at 375F.

Per Serving: 351 calories,17.1g protein, 41.6g carbohydrates, 13.1g fat, 23.3g fiber , 0mg cholesterol, 29mg sodium, 567mg potassium.

Corn Patties

Yield: 4 servings | **Prep Time:** 15 minutes | **Cook Time:** 10 minutes

Ingredients:

- ½ cup chickpeas, cooked
- 1 cup corn kernels, cooked
- 1 tablespoon fresh parsley, chopped
- 1 teaspoon chili powder
- ½ teaspoon ground coriander
- 1 tablespoon tomato paste
- 1 tablespoon almond meal
- 1 tablespoon olive oil

Instructions:

1. Mash the cooked chickpeas and combine them with corn kernels, parsley, chili powder, ground coriander, tomato paste, and almond meal.

2. Stir the mixture until homogenous. 3. Make the small patties.

4. After this, heat up olive oil in the skillet.

5. Put the prepared patties in the hot oil and cook them for 3 minutes per side or until they are golden brown.

6. Dry the cooked patties with the help of the paper towel if needed.

Per Serving: 168 calories,6.7g protein, 23.9g carbohydrates, 6.3g fat, 6g fiber, 0mg cholesterol, 23mg sodium, 392mg potassium.

Tofu Stir Fry

Yield: 3 servings | **Prep Time:** 15 minutes | **Cook Time:** 10 minutes

Ingredients:

- 9 oz firm tofu, cubed
- 3 tablespoons low-sodium soy sauce
- 1 teaspoon sesame seeds
- 1 tablespoon sesame oil
- 1 cup spinach, chopped
- ¼ cup of water

Instructions:

1. In the mixing bowl mix up soy sauce, and sesame oil.

2. Dip the tofu cubes in the soy sauce mixture and leave for 10 minutes to marinate.

3. Heat up a skillet and put the tofu cubes inside. Roast them for 1.5 minutes from each side.

4. Then add water, remaining soy sauce mixture, and chopped spinach.

5. Close the lid and cook the meal for 5 minutes more.

Per Serving: 118 calories, 8.5g protein, 3.1g carbohydrates, 8.6g fat, 1.1g fiber, 0mg cholesterol, 406mg sodium, 193mg potassium.

Briam

Yield: 4 servings | **Prep Time:** 20 minutes | **Cook Time:** 55 minutes

Ingredients:

- 2 zucchinis, sliced
- 2 potatoes, sliced
- 1 red onion, sliced
- 1 teaspoon dried oregano
- ½ teaspoon dried rosemary
- ½ cup fresh cilantro, chopped
- 1 cup marinara sauce
- 1 tablespoon olive oil

Instructions:

1. Mix up zucchinis, potatoes, and onion in the bowl.

2. Sprinkle the vegetables with dried oregano, rosemary, and cilantro.

3. Add olive oil and shake the vegetables well.

4. Then place them one-by-one in the baking pan and top with marinara sauce.

5. Cover the vegetables with foil and bake in the preheated to 385F oven for 55 minutes.

Per Serving: 187 calories,4.5g protein, 31.6g carbohydrates, 5.6g fat, 6.1g fiber, 1 mg cholesterol, 275mg sodium, 946mg potassium.

Dill Zucchini Patties

Yield: 6 servings | **Prep Time:** 10 minutes | **Cook Time:** 10 minutes

Ingredients:

- 3 cups zucchinis, grated
- ½ cup fresh dill, chopped
- ½ cup oatmeal, grinded
- 1 tablespoon dairy-free yogurt
- 1 teaspoon ground black pepper
- 1 tablespoon canola oil

Instructions:

1. Mix up grated zucchini, dill, yogurt, and ground black pepper. 2. Then add oatmeal and stir the mixture until homogenous.

3. Heat up canola oil in the skillet for 2 minutes.

4. Make the patties with the help of the spoon and put them in the hot oil.

5. Cook the patties for 4 minutes per side or until patties are golden brown.

Per Serving: 67 calories, 2.4g protein, 9g carbohydrates, 3.1g fat, 1.9g fiber, 0mg cholesterol, 15mg sodium, 309mg potassium.

Zucchini Grinders

Yield: 2 serving | **Prep Time:** 10 minutes | **Cook Time:** 20 minutes

Ingredients:

- 1 zucchini, diced
- ¼ cup marinara sauce
- 2 oz vegan mozzarella, grated
- 1 teaspoon olive oil
- 1 teaspoon chili powder

Instructions:

1. Roast the zucchini in olive oil for 4 minutes. Stir the vegetables occasionally.

2. After this, transfer the vegetables in the baking pan flatten well. 3. Add marinar a sauce and mozzarella.

4. Cover it with foil and bake for 15 minutes at 365F.

Per Serving: 157 calories,2.9g protein, 15.3g carbohydrates, 9.6g fat, 2.3g fiber, 1 mg cholesterol, 361mg sodium, 380mg potassium.

Pakoras

Yield: 3 servings | **Prep Time:** 15 minutes | **Cook Time:** 14 minutes

Ingredients:

- 1 potato, diced
- 1 onion, diced
- 1 tablespoon cilantro, chopped
- ½ cup chickpea flour
- 1 teaspoon chili flakes
- ¼ cup whole-grain wheat flour
- 4 tablespoons water
- 1 tablespoon olive oil

Instructions:

1. Mix up the potato, onion, cilantro, chickpea flour, chili flakes, wheat flour, and water.

2. Make the homogenous mixture.

3. Then heat up olive oil in the skillet.

4. Make the small pakoras with the help of the spoon and put them in the hot oil.

5. Roast the pakoras for 3.5 minutes per side on the medium heat or until they are golden brown.

6. Dry the cooked meal with the help of the paper towel.

Per Serving: 254 calories,9.4g protein, 40.8g carbohydrates, 7g fat, 9.1g fiber, 0mg cholesterol, 14mg sodium, 627mg potassium.

Desserts Savory Fruit Salad

Yield: 2 servings | **Prep Time:** 10 minutes | **Cook Time:** 0 minutes

Ingredients:

- ½ cup strawberries halves
- ½ cup grapes, halved
- 4 oz mango, chopped
- ¼ cup fat-free yogurt
- 1 teaspoon lime zest, grated
- 1 tablespoon liquid honey

Instructions:

1. In the salad bowl mix up strawberries, grapes, mango, and lime zest.

2. Then add yogurt and sprinkle the salad with liquid honey. 3. Shake it gently.

Per Serving: 110 calories, 2.7g protein, 26.4g carbohydrates, 0.5g fat, 2g fiber, 1mg cholesterol, 25mg sodium, 279mg potassium.

Beans Brownies

Yield: 6 servings | **Prep Time:** 15 minutes | **Cook Time:** 15 minutes

Ingredients:

- 1 cup black beans, cooked
- 1 tablespoon cocoa powder
- 5 oz quick oats
- 3 tablespoons of liquid honey
- 1 teaspoon baking powder
- 1 tablespoon lemon juice
- 1 teaspoon vanilla extract
- 1 teaspoon olive oil

Instructions:

1. Mash the black beans until smooth and mix them up with cocoa powder, quick o ats, honey, baking powder, lemon juice, and vanilla extract.

2. Add olive oil and stir the mass with the help of the spoon.

3. Then line the baking pan with baking paper.

4. Transfer the brownie mixture in the baking pan and flatten it well. Cut the bro wnie into the bars.

5. Bake the dessert in the preheated to 360F oven for 15 minutes.

6. Cool the cooked brownies well.

Per Serving: 244 calories,10.3g protein, 45.8g carbohydrates, 2.9g fat, 7.6g fiber, 0 mg cholesterol, 5mg sodium, 681mg potassium.

Avocado Mousse

Yield: 2 servings | **Prep Time:** 10 minutes | **Cook Time:** 0 minutes

Ingredients:

- 1 avocado, peeled, pitted
- ½ cup low-fat milk
- 1 teaspoon vanilla extract
- 1 tablespoon cocoa powder
- 2 teaspoons liquid honey

Instructions:

1. Chop avocado and putt it in the food processor.

2. Add milk, vanilla extract, and cocoa powder.

3. Blend the mixture until smooth.

4. Pour the cooked mousse in the glasses and top with honey.

Per Serving: 264 calories,4.5g protein, 19.2g carbohydrates, 20.5g fat, 7.5g fiber, 3 mg cholesterol, 34mg sodium, 653mg potassium.

Fruit Kebabs

Yield: 3 servings | **Prep Time:** 10 minutes | **Cook Time:** 0 minutes

Ingredients:

- 1 cup strawberries
- 1 cup melon, cubed
- 1 cup grapes
- 2 kiwis, cubed
- 1 cup watermelon, cubed

Instructions:

1. String the fruits in the wooden skewers one-by-one.

2. Store the cooked fruit kebabs in the fridge, not more than 30 minutes.

Per Serving: 100 calories,1.8g protein, 24.4g carbohydrates, 0.7g fat, 3.4g fiber, 0 mg cholesterol, 12mg sodium, 485mg potassium.

Vanilla Soufflé

Yield: 2 servings | **Prep Time:** 10 minutes | **Cook Time:** 30 minutes

Ingredients:

- 2 egg yolks, whisked
- 2 tablespoons whole-grain wheat flour
- 1 teaspoon vanilla extract
- 1 tablespoon potato starch
- 2 tablespoons agave nectar
- 1 cup low-fat milk

Instructions:

1. Mix up milk and egg yolks.

2. Add vanilla extract, flour, and potato starch.

3. Whisk the liquid until smooth and bring it to boil.

4. Add agave syrup and stir well.

5. Then pour the mixture into the soufflé ramekins and transfer in the preheated t o 350F oven.

6. Bake soufflé for 15 minutes.

Per Serving: 139 calories,7.8g protein, 12.9g carbohydrates, 5.8g fat, 0.9g fiber, 21 6mg cholesterol, 62mg sodium, 235mg potassium.

Strawberries in Dark Chocolate

Yield: 2 servings | **Prep Time:** 15 minutes | **Cook Time:** 1 minute

Ingredients:

- 1 cup strawberries
- 1 tablespoon olive oil
- 1 oz dark chocolate, chopped

Instructions:

1. Melt the chocolate in the microwave oven for 10 seconds. If it is not enough, repe at 10 seconds again.

2. Then mix up chocolate and olive oil. Whisk well.

3. Freeze the strawberries for 10 minutes in the freezer.

4. Then sprinkle them with chocolate mixture.

Per Serving: 159 calories,1.6g protein, 14g carbohydrates, 11.4g fat, 1.9g fiber, 3m g cholesterol, 12mg sodium, 163mg potassium.

Fruit Bowl

Yield: 4 servings | **Prep Time:** 10 minutes | **Cook Time:**0 minutes

Ingredients:

- 1 pitaya, peeled, chopped

- 2 kiwis, chopped
- 2 bananas, chopped
- ½ cup mango, chopped
- 1 teaspoon chia seeds
- 1 teaspoon coconut flakes

Instructions:

1. Mix up pitaya, kiwis, bananas, and mango in the big bowl.

2. Then transfer the mixture into the serving bowls and sprinkle with chia seeds and coconut flakes.

Per Serving: 112 calories,1.7g protein, 26.1g carbohydrates, 1.3g fat, 3.9g fiber, 0 mg cholesterol, 3mg sodium, 373mg potassium.

Berry Smoothie

Yield: 2 servings | **Prep Time:** 5 minutes | **Cook Time:** 0 minutes

Ingredients:

- 1 cup blackberries
- 1 cup strawberries
- 1 cup blueberries
- 1 cup low-fat yogurt

Instructions:

1. Put all ingredients in the blender and blend until you get a smooth mixture.

2. Pour the cooked smoothie in the glasses.

Per Serving: 183 calories,9g protein, 31.6g carbohydrates, 2.3g fat, 7g fiber, 7mg cholesterol, 88mg sodium, 569mg potassium.

Grilled Peaches

Yield: 4 servings | **Prep Time:** 10 minutes | **Cook Time:** 4 minutes

Ingredients:

- 8 peaches, pitted, halved
- 1 teaspoon canola oil
- ½ teaspoon ground cinnamon

Instructions:

1. Preheat the grill to 395F.

2. Meanwhile, sprinkle the peaches with ground cinnamon and canola oil.

3. Put the fruits in the grill and roast them for 2 minutes per side or until the peaches are tender.

Per Serving: 129 calories,2.8g protein, 28.2g carbohydrates, 2g fat, 4.8g fiber, 0mg cholesterol, 0mg sodium, 571mg potassium.

Stuffed Fruits

Yield: 3 servings | **Prep Time:** 10 minutes | **Cook Time:** 0 minutes

Ingredients:

- 3 figs, raw
- 3 teaspoons low-fat goat cheese
- 1 tablespoon liquid honey
- 3 walnuts

Instructions:

1. Make the cross on the top of every fig and scoop a small amount of the fig meat from them.

2. Then fill the figs with low-
fat goat cheese and walnuts. 3. Sprinkle the fruits with liquid honey.

Per Serving: 203 calories,6.6g protein, 19.2g carbohydrates, 11.9g fat, 2.9g fiber, 15mg cholesterol, 51mg sodium, 140mg potassium.

Oatmeal Cookies

Yield: 4 servings | **Prep Time:** 10 minutes | **Cook Time:** 15 minutes

Ingredients:

- 1 cup oatmeal, grinded
- 1 teaspoon vanilla extract
- 1 teaspoon honey
- 3 bananas, mashed

Instructions:

1. Mix up mashed bananas and oatmeal.

2. Add vanilla extract and honey. Stir the mixture well. 3. Then line the baking tray with baking paper.

4. Make the small cookies from the banana mixture with the help of the spoon and put them in the prepared baking tray.

5. Bake the cookies for 15 minutes at 360F or until the cookies are light brown.

Per Serving: 165 calories,3.7g protein, 35.6g carbohydrates, 1.6g fat, 4.4g fiber, 0 mg cholesterol, 2mg sodium, 393mg potassium.

Baked Apples

Yield: 3 servings | **Prep Time:** 10 minutes | **Cook Time:** 35 minutes

Ingredients:

- 3 apples
- 3 pecans, chopped

- 1 tablespoon raisins, chopped
- 3 teaspoons liquid honey
- ½ teaspoon ground cardamom

Instructions:

1. Scoop the tops of the apples to get the medium size holes.

2. Then fill the holes with pecans, raisins, and ground cardamom. 3. Add liquid honey and wrap the apples in the foil (separately –wrap each apple).

4. Bake the apples in the preheated to 380F oven for 35 minutes.

Per Serving: 245 calories,2.3g protein, 41.2g carbohydrates, 10.4g fat, 7.1g fiber, 0 mg cholesterol, 3mg sodium, 327mg potassium.

Peach Crumble

Yield: 2 servings | **Prep Time:** 15 minutes | **Cook Time:** 25 minutes

Ingredients:

- 1 cup peach, chopped
- 1 teaspoon ground nutmeg
- ½ teaspoon ground cinnamon
- 2 tablespoons margarine, softened
- 4 tablespoons oatmeal, grinded
- 1 teaspoon olive oil

Instructions:

1. Mix up margarine and oatmeal. When you get a smooth dough, crumble the mixture with the help of the fingertips.

2. After this, brush the small baking pan with olive oil and put the peaches inside.

3. Sprinkle the peaches with ground nutmeg and ground cinnamon.

4. After this, top the fruits with crumbled dough.

5. Bake the meal for 25 minutes at 360F or until you get the light brown crust.

Per Serving: 197 calories,2.3g protein, 15.1g carbohydrates, 15g fat, 2.7g fiber, 0mg cholesterol, 134mg sodium, 192mg potassium.

Banana Saute

Yield: 2 servings | **Prep Time:** 5 minutes | **Cook Time:** 5 minutes

Ingredients:

- 2 bananas, peeled
- 2 tablespoons orange juice
- 1 tablespoon margarine

Instructions:

1. Slice the bananas lengthwise.

2. Toss the margarine in the skillet and melt it.

3. Put the sliced bananas in the hot margarine and sprinkle with orange juice.

4. Saute the fruits for 2 minutes per side on medium heat.

Per Serving: 163 calories,1.5g protein, 28.6g carbohydrates, 6.1g fat, 3.1g fiber, 0 mg cholesterol, 68mg sodium, 456mg potassium.

Rhubarb Muffins

Yield: 4 servings | **Prep Time:** 10 minutes | **Cook Time:** 15 minutes

Ingredients:

- 1 cup rhubarb, diced
- ¼ cup applesauce
- 1 egg, beaten
- 1 teaspoon baking powder
- 1 cup whole-wheat flour
- 1 tablespoon avocado oil
- 1 teaspoon lemon zest, grated
- ½ cup low-fat yogurt
- 2 tablespoons of liquid honey

Instructions:

1. In the mixing bowl, mix up applesauce, egg, baking powder, flour, avocado oil, le mon zest, honey, and yogurt.

2. When you get the smooth texture of the mass, add rhubarb and stir it well with the help of the spoon.

3. Preheat the oven to 365F.

4. Fill ½ part of every muffin mold with rhubarb batter and transfer them in the o ven.

5. Bake the muffins for 15 minutes.

Per Serving: 202 calories,6.7g protein, 38.7g carbohydrates, 2.3g fat, 1.8g fiber, 43 mg cholesterol, 41mg sodium, 363mg potassium.

Poached Pears

Yield: 6 servings | **Prep Time:** 5 minutes | **Cook Time:** 35 minutes

Ingredients:

- 6 pears, peeled
- 3 cups orange juice
- 1 teaspoon cardamom
- 1 cinnamon stick
- 1 anise star

Instructions:

1. In the saucepan mix up orange juice, cardamom, cinnamon stick, and anise star.

2. Bring the liquid to boil.

3. Add peeled pears and close the lid.

4. Cook the fruits for 25 minutes on the medium heat.

Per Serving: 178 calories,1.6g protein, 45g carbohydrates, 0.6g fat, 6.8g fiber, 0mg cholesterol, 4mg sodium, 494mg potassium.

Lemon Pie

Yield: 8 servings | **Prep Time:** 15 minutes | **Cook Time:** 15 minutes

Ingredients:

- 1 pie crust
- ¼ cup lemon juice
- ½ cup low-fat milk
- 3 egg yolks
- 2 tablespoons potato starch

Instructions:

1. Pour milk in the saucepan.

2. Add starch, egg yolks, and lemon juice. 3. Whisk the liquid until smooth.

4. Simmer it for 6 minutes. Stir it constantly.

5. Then leave the mixture for 10-15 minutes to cool.

6. Pour the lemon mixture over the pie crust and flatten it well.

Per Serving: 181 calories,2.8g protein, 21.9g carbohydrates, 9.3g fat, 0.5g fiber, 79 mg cholesterol, 182mg sodium, 66mg potassium.

Cardamom Pudding

Yield: 2 servings | **Prep Time:** 20 minutes | **Cook Time:** 10 minutes

Ingredients:

- 1 cup of coconut milk
- 1 teaspoon agar agar
- 1 teaspoon ground cardamom
- 1 teaspoon vanilla extract
- 1 teaspoon honey

Instructions:

1. Pour coconut milk in the saucepan.

2. Add agar, ground cardamom, and vanilla extract. Whisk the liquid until smooth.

3. Bring it to boil and simmer for 5 minutes on the low heat.

4. Then remove the pudding from heat and leave for 10 minutes to cool.

5. Add honey and stir well.

6. Transfer the pudding in the serving cups and leave for 10 minutes in the fridge.

Per Serving: 296 calories,2.9g protein, 10.7g carbohydrates, 28.7g fat, 3.1g fiber, 0 mg cholesterol, 20mg sodium, 333mg potassium.

Banana Bread

Yield: 6 servings | **Prep Time:** 15 minutes | **Cook Time:** 45 minutes

Ingredients:

- ½ cup low-fat sour cream
- 2 bananas, mashed
- 1 teaspoon baking powder
- 1 teaspoon apple cider vinegar
- 1 egg, beaten
- ½ cup oatmeal, grinded

- ¼ cup whole-wheat flour
- 2 tablespoons margarine, melted

Instructions:

1. Mix up all ingredients and whisk the mixture until smooth. 2. Then preheat the oven to 360F.

3. Pour the banana bread mixture in the loaf mold and flatten well.

4. Bake the banana bread in the oven for 45 minutes.

5. Cool the cooked bread well, remove it from the loaf mold and slice into the servings.

Per Serving: 166 calories,3.4g protein, 18.9g carbohydrates, 9.2g fat, 1.9g fiber, 36 mg cholesterol, 66mg sodium, 295mg potassium.

Banana Split

Yield: 2 servings | **Prep Time:** 10 minutes | **Cook Time:** 0 minutes

Ingredients:

- 2 bananas, peeled
- 2 tablespoons pineapple, chopped
- 2 tablespoons low-fat yogurt
- 1 teaspoon liquid honey
- 2 tablespoons granola cereals

Instructions:

1. Cut every banana lengthwise and place it in the serving plates. 2. Top the fruits with granola cereals, yogurt, and pineapple.

3. Then sprinkle the bananas with liquid honey.

Per Serving: 149 calories,4.5g protein, 40.4g carbohydrates,4.3g fat, 4.6g fiber, 1mg cholesterol, 16mg sodium, 554mg potassium.

Mint Parfait

Yield: 2 servings | **Prep Time:** 10 minutes | **Cook Time:** 0 minutes

Ingredients:

- 2 cups low-fat yogurt
- 1 teaspoon liquid honey
- 2 teaspoons lime zest, grated
- 4 oranges, peeled and chopped
- 1 tablespoon mint, chopped

Instructions:

1. Mix up all ingredients in the bowl.

2. Then transfer the dessert in the serving bowls.

Per Serving: 360 calories, 17.5g protein, 63.9g carbohydrates, 3.5g fat, 9.2g fiber, 15mg cholesterol, 173mg sodium, 1257mg potassium.

Pudding Dessert

Yield: 4 servings | **Prep Time:** 10 minutes | **Cook Time:** 24 minutes

Ingredients:

- 1 cup strawberries
- 1 tablespoon honey
- 4 eggs, beaten
- 1 tablespoon potato starch
- 2 cups low-fat milk

Instructions:

1. In a bowl, combine the strawberries with the honey and all remaining ingredients.

2. Pour the mixture in the ramekins and transfer in the oven. 3. Bake the pudding for 24 minutes at 375F.

Per Serving: 152 calories,9.9g protein, 16g carbohydrates, 5.7g fat, 0.7g fiber, 170 mg cholesterol, 116mg sodium, 300mg potassium.

Vanilla Chocolate Brownie

Yield: 8 servings | **Prep Time:** 10 minutes | **Cook Time:** 30 minutes

Ingredients:

- 1 tablespoon cocoa powder
- 4 egg whites, whisked
- ½ cup hot water
- 1 teaspoon vanilla extract
- 1 teaspoon baking powder
- 1 cup whole-wheat flour
- 2 tablespoons of liquid honey
- 1 teaspoon margarine, softened Cooking spray

Instructions:

1. In the mixing bowl, mix up all ingredients and whisk them until smooth.

2. In another bowl, combine the sugar with flour, baking powder and walnuts and stir.

3. Pour the mixture into a cake pan greased with cooking spray, flatten well, bake i n the oven for 30 minutes, cool down, cut into bars, and serve.

Per Serving: 89 calories, 3.6g protein, 17.1g carbohydrates, 0.7g fat, 0.6g fiber, 0m g cholesterol, 24mg sodium, 128mg potassium.

Walnut Pie

Yield: 8 servings | **Prep Time:** 10 minutes | **Cook Time:** 25 minutes

Ingredients:

- 3 cups almond flour
- 1 tablespoon vanilla extract
- ½ cup walnuts, chopped
- 2 teaspoons baking soda 1 cup low-fat milk
- 1 egg, beaten
- 1 teaspoon liquid honey, for decoration

Instructions:

1. Mix up all ingredients except honey in the bowl and pour the mixture in the baking pan.

3. Bake the pie in the oven at 370F for 25 minutes.

4. Leave the cake to cool down, sprinkle with honey, and cut into servings.

Per Serving: 134 calories, 5.9g protein, 4.8g carbohydrates, 10.7g fat, 1.7g fiber, 2 2mg cholesterol, 340mg sodium, 96mg potassium.

Milk Fudge

Yield: 12 servings | **Prep Time:** 120 minutes | **Cook Time:** 7 minutes

Ingredients:

- 1 cup low-fat milk
- ½ cup margarine
- ½ cup of cocoa powder
- 1 teaspoon vanilla extract

Instructions:

1. Heat up a pan with the milk over medium heat, add the margarine, stir and cook everything for 7 minutes.

2. Take this off heat, add the cocoa powder and whisk well. 3. Pour the mixture int o a lined square pan, flatten ell and refrigerate in the fridge for 120 minutes.

Per Serving: 85 calories, 1.4g protein, 3.1g carbohydrates, 8.2g fat, 1.1g fiber, 1mg cholesterol, 98mg sodium, 125mg potassium.

Charlotte Pie

Yield: 4 servings | **Prep Time:** 10 minutes | **Cook Time:** 30 minutes

Ingredients:

- 2 cups almond flour
- 1 teaspoon baking powder
- ½ teaspoon ground cinnamon
- 1 tablespoon honey
- ½ cup low-fat milk
- 1 cup apples, chopped Cooking spray

Instructions:

1. Mix up almond flour, baking powder, cinnamon, honey, and milk in the bowl.

2. Whisk the mixture well and add apples.

3. Then pour this mixture into a cake pan greased with the cooking spray, flatten well and bake in the oven at 360F for 30 minutes.

4. Cool the pie down, slice and serve.

Per Serving: 140 calories, 4.2g protein, 17.4g carbohydrates, 7.4g fat, 3g fiber, 2m g cholesterol, 20mg sodium, 236mg potassium.

Kiwi Salad

Yield: 8 servings | **Prep Time:** 10 minutes | **Cook Time:** 0 minutes

Ingredients:

- 1 watermelon, chopped
- 1 cup raspberries, chopped
- 2 cups kiwis, peeled and chopped
- 8 ounces low-fat yogurt

Instructions:

1. Mix up all ingredients in the salad bowl and shake well.

Per Serving: 60 calories, 2.4g protein, 11.5g carbohydrates, 0.7g fat, 2.4g fiber, 2mg cholesterol, 22mg sodium, 245mg potassium.

Vanilla Cream

Yield: 4 servings | **Prep Time:** 120 minutes | **Cook Time:** 10 minutes

Ingredients:

- 1 cup low-fat milk
- 1 cup fat-free cream cheese
- 1 teaspoon vanilla extract
- 2 tablespoons corn starch
- 4 teaspoons liquid honey

Instructions:

1. Heat up a pan with the milk over medium heat, add the rest of the ingredients, whisk, and cook for 10 minutes on low heat.

2. Divide the mix into bowls and refrigerate the cream for 120 minutes in the fridge.

Per Serving: 123 calories,10.4g protein, 16.8g carbohydrates,1.4g fat, 0g fiber, 8mg cholesterol, 343mg sodium, 191mg potassium.

Mousse with Coconut

Yield: 12 servings | **Prep Time:** 10 minutes | **Cook Time:** 5 minutes

Ingredients:

- 3 cups low-fat milk
- 2 tablespoons coconut flakes
- 3 tablespoons corn starch
- 3 tablespoons of liquid honey

Instructions:

1. Bring the milk to boil and add coconut flakes and corn starch.

2. Simmer the mousse for 2 minutes.

3. Cool the dessert and mix it up with liquid honey.

Per Serving: 53 calories, 2.1g protein, 9.8g carbohydrates, 0.9g fat, 0.1g fiber, 3mg cholesterol, 27mg sodium, 97mg potassium.

Pecan Brownies

Yield: 8 servings | **Prep Time:** 10 minutes | **Cook Time:** 25 minutes

Ingredients:

- 5 pecans, chopped
- 2 tablespoons cocoa powder
- 2 eggs, beaten
- 2 tablespoons margarine, softened
- ½ teaspoon baking powder
- 1 cup almond meal Cooking spray

Instructions:

1. In your food processor, mix up all ingredients except cooking spray.

2. Then spray the square pan with cooking spray, add the brownies batter, flatten i t, and transfer in the oven, bake it at 350F for 25 minutes.

3. Cool the cooked brownies and cut into bars.

Per Serving: 174 calories, 5g protein, 4.8g carbohydrates, 16.3g fat, 2.8g fiber, 41 mg cholesterol, 49mg sodium, 205mg potassium.

Mango Rice

Yield: 4 servings | **Prep Time:** 10 minutes | **Cook Time:** 30 minutes

Ingredients:

- ½ cup of rice
- 2 cups low-fat milk
- 1 mango, peeled and chopped
- 1 teaspoon vanilla extract
- ½ teaspoon ground cinnamon

Instructions:

1. Bring the milk to a boil and add rice.

2. Simmer it for 25 minutes.

3. Add vanilla, cinnamon, and mango, stir and cool to the room temperature.

Per Serving: 190 calories,6.5g protein, 37.5g carbohydrates,1.7g fat, 1.8g fiber, 6mg cholesterol, 56mg sodium, 354mg potassium.

Strawberry Pie

Yield: 6 servings | **Prep Time:** 10 minutes | **Cook Time:** 25 minutes

Ingredients:

- 2 cups whole wheat flour
- 1 cup strawberries, chopped
- ½ teaspoon baking powder
- ½ cup low-fat milk

- 2 tablespoons margarine, softened
- 1 tablespoon coconut flakes
- 2 eggs, beaten
- 1 teaspoon vanilla extract

Instructions:

1. In a bowl, combine the flour with the strawberries and all the ingredients from the list above.

3. Pour the strawberry batter in the baking pan, flatten well, and cook in the preheated to 365F oven for 25 minutes.

Per Serving: 228 calories, 7.1g protein, 35.2g carbohydrates, 6.2g fat, 1.7g fiber, 56mg cholesterol, 75mg sodium, 180mg potassium.

Cream Cheese Pie

Yield: 12 servings | **Prep Time:** 10 minutes | **Cook Time:** 25 minutes=

Ingredients:

- 2 cups whole wheat flour
- 4 tablespoons margarine, melted
- 1 cup low-fat cream cheese
- 1 teaspoon vanilla extract
- 1 egg, beaten
- 2 tablespoons of liquid honey
- 1 teaspoon baking powder

Instructions:

1. In a bowl, combine the flour with the margarine, and cream cheese.

2. Add egg, vanilla extract, baking powder, and honey. Stir the mixture until smooth,

3. Transfer the batter in the round pan, flatten well and bake in the oven at 350F for 20 minutes.

4. Cool the pie well.

Per Serving: 194 calories,4.1g protein, 19,6g carbohydrates,11,1g fat, 0.6g fiber, 3 5mg cholesterol, 108mg sodium, 97mg potassium.

Ginger Cream

Yield: 5 servings | **Prep Time:** 10 minutes | **Cook Time:** 0 minutes

Ingredients:

- 3 cups non-fat milk
- 1 teaspoon ginger, ground
- 2 teaspoons vanilla extract
- 1 cup nuts, chopped

Instructions:

1. Blend the nuts until smooth and mix them up with ginger, milk, and vanilla extract. Stir well.

Per Serving: 223 calories,9.6g protein, 14.6g carbohydrates,14.1g fat, 2.5g fiber, 3 mg cholesterol, 262mg sodium, 399mg potassium.

Raspberry Stew

Yield: 6 servings | **Prep Time:** 10 minutes | **Cook Time:** 10 minutes

Ingredients:

- 16 ounces raspberries
- 2 tablespoons water
- 2 tablespoons lime juice
- ¼ teaspoon lime zest, grated
- 2 tablespoons cornstarch

Instructions:

1. Put all ingredients except cornstarch in the saucepan and bring to boil.

2. Add cornstarch stir until it is smooth and cook for 2 minutes more.

Per Serving: 51 calories, 0.9g protein, 11.8g carbohydrates,0.5g fat, 5g fiber, 0mg cholesterol, 2mg sodium, 118mg potassium.

Melon Salad

Yield: 4 servings | **Prep Time:** 4 minutes | **Cook Time:** 0 minutes

Ingredients:

- 1 cup melon, chopped
- 2 bananas, chopped
- 1 tablespoon low-fat cream cheese

Instructions:

1. Mix up all ingredients and transfer them to the serving plates.

Per Serving: 75 calories,1.2g protein, 16.7g carbohydrates,1.1g fat, 1.9g fiber, 3mg cholesterol, 14mg sodium, 318mg potassium.

Rhubarb with Aromatic Mint

Yield: 4 servings | **Prep Time:** 10 minutes | **Cook Time:** 10 minutes

Ingredients:

- ¼ cup low-fat milk
- 2 cups rhubarb, roughly chopped
- 1 tablespoon liquid honey
- 1 tablespoon mint, chopped

Instructions:

1. Bring the milk to boil, add mint and rhubarb.

2. Cook the dessert for 10 minutes over the low heat. 3. Then cool the meal and add liquid honey. Stir it.

Per Serving: 36 calories,1.1g protein, 8g carbohydrates,0.3g fat, 1.2g fiber, 1mg cholesterol, 10mg sodium, 208mg potassium.

Lime Pears

Yield: 2 servings | **Prep Time:** 10 minutes | **Cook Time:** 15 minutes

Ingredients:

- 2 teaspoons lime juice
- 1 teaspoon lime zest
- 4 pears, cored and cubed
- 1 tablespoon margarine

Instructions:

3. Bake the pears in the preheated to 375F oven for 15 minutes.

4. Meanwhile, melt the margarine and mix it up with line zest and

lime juice.

5. When the pears are baked, sprinkle them with lime juice mixture.

Per Serving: 148 calories,0.8g protein, 32.5g carbohydrates,3.2g fat, 6.6g fiber, 0mg cholesterol, 37mg sodium, 251mg potassium.

Nigella Mix

Yield: 8 servings | **Prep Time:** 10 minutes | **Cook Time:** 10 minutes

Ingredients:

- 4 cups mango, chopped
- 1 teaspoon nigella seeds
- 1 teaspoon vanilla extract
- ½ cup apple juice
- 1 teaspoon cinnamon powder

Instructions:

1. Mix up all ingredients together and transfer them in the serving bowls.

Per Serving: 64 calories,0.7 protein, 14.2g carbohydrates,1g fat, 1.4g fiber, 0mg cholesterol, 2mg sodium, 155mg potassium.

Peach Stew

Yield: 4 servings | **Prep Time:** 10 minutes | **Cook Time:** 15 minutes

Ingredients:

- 2 cups peaches, halved
- 2 cups of water
- 1 tablespoon honey
- 2 tablespoons lemon juice

Instructions:

1. Mix up all ingredients in the saucepan and simmer for 15 minutes over the low heat.

Per Serving: 47 calories,0.8g protein, 11.5g carbohydrates,0.3g fat, 1.2g fiber, 0mg cholesterol, 5mg sodium, 156mg potassium.

Berry Curd

Yield: 2 servings | **Prep Time:** 10 minutes | **Cook Time:** 10 minutes

Ingredients:

- 2 tablespoons lime juice
- 1 tablespoon margarine
- 12 ounces blueberries
- 1 tablespoon cornstarch

Instructions:

1. Put all ingredients except cornstarch in the saucepan and bring to boil.

2. Then blend the berries with the help of the immersion blender and add cornstarch. Simmer the curd for 3 minutes more.

Per Serving: 167 calories,1.4g protein, 29.4g carbohydrates,6.3g fat, 4.2g fiber, 0mg cholesterol, 70mg sodium, 146mg potassium.

Cantaloupe Mix

Yield: 4 servings | **Prep Time:** 10 minutes | **Cook Time:** 0 minutes

Ingredients:

- 2 cups cantaloupe, chopped
- 2 teaspoons vanilla extract
- 2 teaspoons orange juice

Instructions:

1. Mix up all ingredients in the bowl and leave for 5 minutes.

2. Then transfer the dessert in the serving plates.

Per Serving: 34 calories,0.7g protein, 6.9g carbohydrates,0.2g fat, 0.7g fiber, 0mg cholesterol, 13mg sodium, 217mg potassium.

Lime Cream

Yield: 4 servings | **Prep Time:** 10 minutes | **Cook Time:** 15 minutes

Ingredients:

- 3 cups low-fat milk
- ½ cup lime juice
- 1 teaspoon lime zest, grated
- ½ cup agave syrup
- 2 tablespoons potato starch

Instructions:

1. Heat up milk and add lime zest, agave syrup, and potato starch.

2. Simmer the liquid for 5 minutes more. Stir ti constantly.

3. Then cool the milk mixture, add lime juice, and stir well.

Per Serving: 230 calories,6.3g protein, 49.4g carbohydrates,1.9g fat, 0.2g fiber, 9mg cholesterol, 114mg sodium, 323 potassium.

Chia and Pineapple Bowl

Yield: 4 servings | **Prep Time:** 10 minutes | **Cook Time:** 0 minutes

Ingredients:

- 3 cups pineapple, peeled and cubed
- 1 teaspoon chia seeds
- 1 teaspoon fresh mint, chopped
- 1 tablespoon liquid honey

Instructions:

1. Mix up all ingredients in the big bowl.

2. Then transfer the dessert in the serving bowls.

Per Serving: 89 calories,1.1g protein, 21.6g carbohydrates,0.9g fat, 2.6g fiber, 0mg cholesterol, 2mg sodium, 150mg potassium.

Plum Stew

Yield: 4 servings | **Prep Time:** 10 minutes | **Cook Time:** 10 minutes

Ingredients:

- 2 plums, pitted and chopped
- 1 pear, cored and chopped
- 2 tablespoons agave syrup
- ¼ cup coconut, shredded
- 1 tablespoon nuts, chopped
- 1 cup of water

Instructions:

1. In a pan, combine plums, pear, and water.

2. Cook the mixture for 8 minutes, divide into bowls, top with nuts, agave, coconut shred, and serve.

Per Serving: 97 calories,0.9g protein, 19g carbohydrates,2.9g fat, 2.2g fiber, 0mg c holesterol, 23mg sodium, 129mg potassium.

Citrus Pudding

Yield: 4 servings | **Prep Time:** 10 minutes | **Cook Time:** 15 minutes

Ingredients:

- 2 cups orange juice
- 2 tablespoons cornstarch

- ¼ cup of rice
- ¼ cup agave syrup

Instructions:

1. Mix up orange juice and rice in the saucepan and bring it to boil. Simmer the mixture for 10 minutes.

2. Add rice and agave syrup and simmer the pudding for 5 minutes more.

Per Serving: 176 calories,1.6g protein, 42.4g carbohydrates,0.3g fat, 0.4g fiber, 0mg cholesterol, 16mg sodium, 274mg potassium.

Pomegranate Porridge

Yield: 2 servings | **Prep Time:** 5 minutes | **Cook Time:** 8 minutes

Ingredients:

- ¼ cup oatmeal
- 1 cup pomegranate seeds
- 1 cup pomegranate juice

Instructions:

1. Mix up oatmeal and pomegranate juice and simmer the porridge for 5 minutes.

2. Then add pomegranate seeds and stir the porridge well.

Per Serving: 164 calories,1.9g protein, 37.4g carbohydrates,0.7g fat, 1.5g fiber, 0mg cholesterol, 6mg sodium, 337mg potassium.

Apricot Cream

Yield: 4 servings | **Prep Time:** 10 minutes | **Cook Time:** 0 minutes

Ingredients:

- 4 tablespoons cream cheese
- 1 cup apricot, chopped
- 1 teaspoon vanilla extract

Instructions:

1. Blend all ingredients together until you get the creamy texture.

2. Transfer the dessert in the bowls.

Per Serving: 53 calories,1.1g protein, 3.9g carbohydrates,3.6g fat, 0.6g fiber, 11mg cholesterol, 30mg sodium, 85mg potassium.

Cardamom Black Rice Pudding

Yield: 4 servings | **Prep Time:** 10 minutes | **Cook Time:** 20 minutes

Ingredients:

- 5 cups of water
- ½ cup agave syrup
- 2 cups wild rice
- 1 teaspoon ground cardamom

Instructions:

1. Mix up rice, water, and ground cinnamon.

2. Cook the rice for 20 minutes.

3. Add agave syrup and stir the pudding well.

Per Serving: 413 calories,1.8g protein, 93.4g carbohydrates,0.9g fat, 5.1g fiber, 0mg cholesterol, 43mg sodium, 375mg potassium.

Fragrant Apple Halves

Yield: 4 servings | **Prep Time:** 10 minutes | **Cook Time:** 10 minutes

Ingredients:

- 4 apples, halved
- 2 tablespoons chia seeds
- 1 teaspoon vanilla extract
- 1 teaspoon ground cinnamon

Instructions:

1. Rub the apples with vanilla extract and ground cinnamon and transfer in the preheated to 375F oven.

2. Bake the apple halves for 10 minutes.

3. Then sprinkle the apples with chia seeds.

Per Serving: 155 calories,1.8g protein, 34.4g carbohydrates,2.6g fat, 8.2g fiber, 0mg cholesterol, 3mg sodium, 271mg potassium.

CONCLUSION

If you are one of those that cannot live without fried foods, then the best thing you can do is to purchase an air fryer from the nearest store. You will want to air fry your favorite fries, steak, wings, veggies, etc., and not deep fry them. Although research on the impact of air frying foods is limited at the moment, food experts generally recommend limiting the consumption of fried food products.

You should keep in mind that cooking with an air fryer does not always mean that the food is healthful than other cooking methods. Try to include other cooking methods in your dietary routine to ensure optimal health. Other cooking methods you can include in your daily routine include pan-searing, baking, grilling, and oven roasting.

Air frying can significantly lower the number of calories, fat, and other harmful compounds in food compared to oil-frying. Nonetheless, air frying foods can have similar negative health effects just like deep frying if cooking oil is always added and consuming them regularly. Although air frying is considered the best alternative to oil-frying, you will need to reduce eating any fried food products altogether to ensure optimal health.

An air fryer is one of the kitchen appliances you should have in your kitchen. This is because the unit is simple to operate and cooking with and it has significant health benefits. For example, air frying can help you lose some weight. Most brands and models come with components that are non-stick, easy to clean, and dishwasher safe. Lastly, I would recommend you to try out the recipes in this book and also share what you learn with your colleagues and friends. I thank all of you who have read this cookbook! Enjoy!

Printed in Great Britain
by Amazon

25357139R00082